LIVE
WRITING

Other Avon Camelot Books by
Ralph Fletcher

A WRITER'S NOTEBOOK

Avon Books are available at special quantity discounts for bulk purchases for sales promotions, premiums, fund raising or educational use. Special books, or book excerpts, can also be created to fit specific needs.

For details write or telephone the office of the Director of Special Markets, Avon Books, Inc., Dept. FP, 1350 Avenue of the Americas, New York, New York 10019, 1-800-238-0658.

LIVE
WRITING

BREATHING LIFE
INTO YOUR WORDS

RALPH
FLETCHER

AN AVON CAMELOT BOOK

AVON BOOKS, INC.
1350 Avenue of the Americas
New York, New York 10019

Copyright © 1999 by Ralph Fletcher
Published by arrangement with the author
Library of Congress Catalog Card Number: 98-93659
ISBN: 0-380-79701-1
www.avonbooks.com

First Avon Camelot Printing: April 1999

CAMELOT TRADEMARK REG. U.S. PAT. OFF. AND IN OTHER COUNTRIES, MARCA REGISTRADA, HECHO EN U.S.A.

Printed in the U.S.A.

OPM 10 9 8 7 6 5 4 3 2 1

For my son Robert
who inspires me with his original voice and humor

Acknowledgments

Special thanks to the teachers who worked so hard to help me get student samples for my book: Aimee Buckner, Judy Eggemeier, Lynn Herschlein, Miki Maeshiro, Franki Sibberson, Sharon Murray, Jane Theoharides, and Kathy Spryou. Thanks to all the students whose writing appears in these pages: James Albrecht, Melissa Baldassari, Kamele Bento, Athena Biggs, Elissa Bosley, Micah Botelho, Taylor Curtis, Adam Field, Melissa Fitzwater, Leslie Gaillard, Katie Hallinan, Sam Hundt, Dylan Jacobsen, Katie Lathrop, Ashlie McAvene, Noelle Parris, Gina Pedone, Tim Pifer, Zachary Reed, Andy Schlaak, Emma Yuen, Alaysha Vaugn, David Uy, Eric Weeks, Sarah Whitley, Alex Woods, and Jane Wright. Thanks to Elise Howard, Amy Cox, Abby McAden, and Beth Eller at Avon Books. Thanks always to Marian Reiner.

Contents

THE WRITER'S TOOLBOX

My wife gave me a gas grill for Father's Day. I was pleased by this gift until I noticed that all the pieces came packed into a small box.

"It does have to be assembled, but it shouldn't be hard," my wife told me. "The guy at the store said it wouldn't take more than forty-five minutes or so."

I groaned. I have never been much good when it comes to putting stuff together or building things around the house. Saws, tape measures, wrenches, and power tools all give me a bad case of the willies. I usually avoid buying any appliance or toys that have to be put together.

Forty-five minutes, huh? I needed five solid hours to figure out the directions and put the gas grill together.

By the end I practically had smoke coming out of my ears.

My father-in-law, on the other hand, can fix just about anything. The year after I wrestled with that gas grill, he gave me a toolbox as a birthday present. Inside I found three different kinds of screwdrivers, two wrenches, and a set of needlenose pliers.

"It's hard to fix anything without the right tools," he told me. "Every year I'll buy you a few more tools for this toolbox, and I'll show you how to use them. It's not rocket science. Little by little you'll learn."

Here's the most amazing thing: it worked! Now that I had the tools, I could actually fix some simple stuff. No, I'm not about to go out and build a house, but I'm getting better. I'm no longer afraid to repair a screen door or re-place rotted boards on our deck. I'm gaining confidence and even enjoying it once in a while. My father-in-law was right: having the right tools made all the difference.

This book is based on the simple idea that every writer has a toolbox. Instead of awls and hammers, a writer's toolbox contains words, imagination, a love of books, a sense of story, and ideas for how to make the writing live and breathe. I wrote this book to give you some practical strategies to throw into your toolbox. I hope you'll try them, because these are ideas that can make you a better writer.

This book is titled *Live Writing,* and you may be wondering what I mean by that. Most of us have read (and written!) the opposite kind of writing—dull, drab language that is about as interesting to read as a city phone book. By "live writing" I mean the kind of writing that has a current running through it—energy, electricity, juice. When we read live writing, the words seem to lift off the page and burrow deep inside us. My goal in writing this book is to help you make your writing come alive.

Has this ever happened to you? You're in gymnastics class, trying to do a vault for the first time. All the kids are edgy: vaulting looks hard and scary. But one kid looks eager. And when his turn comes, he goes flying toward the vault, hits it, spins into the air, flips over, and lands on his feet. For a second or two everybody watching forgets to breathe.

The ability to vault, ski, hit a golf ball, sing an opera, fix a doorbell, or draw a human figure seems to come easily for certain people. People like that don't seem to struggle or practice like the rest of us; they're just good at whatever it is. We say "She's a natural tennis player" as if that person were born knowing how to breathe, drink milk, and hit a two-handed backhand smash.

The same thing is true for writing. Maybe you've known a boy who can dash off a report at the last minute and still get an A. Or a girl who can write circles around everyone else in the class without even trying. All the stuff most people sweat—organizing ideas, using interesting vocabulary, finding a snappy conclusion—is a cinch for that person. Hanging around such people can become pretty annoying.

Once I was lucky enough to spend a summer day with Cynthia Rylant, who is one of my very favorite writers. Rylant has published many different kinds of writing—poems, picture books, novels—and I was terribly curious about how she goes about the process of writing.

"How often do you have to revise what you've written?" I asked her.

"Oh, I don't revise much at all," she said. "For me it usually comes out right the first time I write it. I guess I'm lucky that way."

I felt like throwing up.

Here's the good news: most of us are not born writers. We were not born with a pencil in our tiny fingers. And very rarely do the words flow clear and sparkling the first time we try to write them down.

Most of us have to work at our writing.

That's the kind of writer I am, and I am not ashamed of it. I'm not a natural. Not a born writer. I have had to work hard to become the kind of writer I want to be. And I'm still not there yet.

I think of myself as a student, a craftsman, an apprentice. Like any apprentice, I know I have to learn my trade the old-fashioned way.

How? First, by writing. A book such as this one can be helpful, but I believe that the best way to learn is by *doing*. I need to be writing on a regular basis, every day if possible. The writer's motto should be: "Never a day without a line of writing."

Second, I seek out books and writers I can learn from. Cynthia Rylant, William Steig, Katherine Paterson, Gary Soto, Ken Kesey, Toni Morrison, and Jack London are just a few of the authors I admire. These writers are vastly different from one another, and I have learned different things from each of them. As I read and reread their books I think of myself as standing right beside their shoulder while they work.

Third, I need ideas about what makes writing work. I care so much about my writing that I want to make it better. But how? How do I craft a lead sentence that will grab my readers? How can I create characters who come to life on the page? How can I let readers get a real sense of where my story is taking place? How can I make my voice, the sound of my writing, natural and authentic?

If you want to improve your writing, this book is for you. Perhaps you like to write but you have the feeling that your writing lacks something. In these pages you'll find dozens of practical tools for improving your writing. We'll break your writing into parts, examine each part, and then help you put it back together again.

Each chapter concerns one particular aspect of writing: beginnings, endings, character, et cetera. The examples I use come mainly from three places: the writing of other young writers like you, writing by published authors, and my own work. These are not just theories; these strategies have made me a much better writer. And you can use them not only in fiction and personal narrative but also in poetry, nonfiction, and even persuasive writing.

HOW TO USE THIS BOOK

There's no one way to read this book. You might decide to read the chapters in sequence. But it could be that you're more interested in sharpening your leads than in creating a sense of place. In that case, you may prefer to skip around and start by reading the chapters in which you're most interested.

You might read the book quickly, cover to cover. But you might find it more useful to stop after you read a chapter, go back to your writing, and actually try out some of the suggested strategies.

Some people read with pen in hand, taking notes as they go along to list ideas, books, excerpts, and so forth. You might consider getting a spiral-bound notebook and dividing it into sections, one section entitled "Voice," one "Conflict," one "Endings," and so forth. That way you can jot down the stuff you might otherwise forget. I sometimes find that copying something down helps me hold it in my head. But *don't* set up this kind of notebook if it feels like a workbook or if you think it might interfere with your reading. Try it only if it makes sense to you.

You probably will not use every one of these writing tools right now. But I hope this will be a book you can read and reread. Hang on to it: an idea you can't use right now may come in handy later.

We live in a world where many people just go out and buy whatever they want—a mountain bike, basketball shoes, even a computer. Learning to write well doesn't come that quickly or easily. The truth is that writing can be hard, and most of us discover that it takes years to become the kind of writer we want to be. As a young writer, you shouldn't get impatient with yourself. This isn't the time for you to worry about winning prizes, writing a best-seller, or getting on *The Oprah Winfrey Show*. This is the time to develop a love of writing, to learn the habits of a writer (keeping a writer's notebook, for example), and to start becoming aware of what makes writing work.

There is no way that your pen will pour out world-class writing every day. Imagine: the best baseball hitters in the world fail to get a hit seven out of ten times at bat! If you can bat .300 in baseball over a whole career, well, you've got a decent shot at getting into the Hall of Fame.

As a writer you have to be willing to strike out more times than you get a hit. Try not to get discouraged. Most of the sentences and paragraphs in my first drafts aren't great; they are just okay. When I reread what I've first written, I find a few places where there is a spark, a hint of something good.

As a writer you have to feed yourself on those sparks. In one story you might write a surprise ending that surprises even you. In another piece you might bring your reader inside a character, into her deepest thoughts, and find that the writing has a new kind of intensity. Apprentice writers build on these beginnings. I have found that even little successes can keep my spirits up for a long time.

Maybe you aren't a natural-born writer like Cynthia Rylant. Or maybe you are one but want to see if you can make your writing even better. In either case, I hope this book gives you a wealth of strategies, ideas, and insider tips to breathe new life into your words, to fuel you for a lifetime of writing.

READING LIKE A WRITER

My brother Joe is a first-rate soccer player; I'm pretty average, and that's being generous. One day Joe took me to a professional soccer game. Right away I could see that we were watching the game differently. I tended to focus on whoever had control of the ball; Joe kept pointing out other players moving into position.

"Look at the way they're always spread out," he said at one point. "They hardly ever bunch up around the ball." And later: "They're great athletes but you notice that they don't wear themselves out running all the time."

I realized that he was watching a different game than I was. We even sat differently. Joe perched on the edge of his seat so he wouldn't miss a thing. He watched carefully because he knew he might pick up some strategy or technique he could use himself while playing soccer. I leaned back, relaxing, basking in the sunlight. I must have figured I could never learn from these pros. They were too good.

I made a mistake that day. And I think we often make the same mistake when we read terrific writing. We read something wonderful and say, "That's too good! I can *never* do that!" But there is always something you can learn from a piece of writing, not matter how impossibly brilliant and accomplished it may be.

Most people read for information or for entertainment. Most readers focus on what is going to happen next.

Not writers. Writers don't read like other people. Writers are interested in what's going to happen, of course, but they are also keenly interested in finding out *how* the author created the effect. That's something you can't always find out on a first reading.

I recently read a short story, "Eleven," by Sandra Cisneros. Here is a passage from the beginning of that story:

What they don't understand about birthdays and what they never tell you is that when you're eleven, you're also ten, and nine, and eight, and seven, and six, and five, and four, and three, and two, and one. And when you wake up on your eleventh birthday you expect to feel eleven, but you don't. You open your eyes and everything's just like yesterday, only it's today. And you don't feel eleven at all. You feel like you're still ten. And you are— underneath the year that makes you eleven.

Like some days you might say something stupid, and that's the part of you that's still ten. Or some days you might need to sit on your mama's lap because you're scared, and that's the part of you that's five. And maybe when you're all grown up maybe you will need to cry like if you're three, and that's okay. That's what I tell Mama when she's sad and needs to cry. Maybe she's feeling three.

Because the way you grow old is kind of like an onion or like the rings inside a tree trunk or like my little wooden dolls that fit one inside the other, one year inside the next. That's how being eleven years old is.

My first reaction: Wow! Such wise words, and so true. Some days I still feel like a little kid. But even as the applause in my head dies down I find myself wondering: How did Sandra Cisneros make this passage work? How does she manage to stir up so many feelings in me with a few simple words? There's not a single fancy four-syllable word in the whole passage.

I need to go back and read the piece again. I notice

the repetition: "And maybe," something I hadn't noticed the first time around. I pay attention to the point of view. She could have written this in the first person ("I open my eyes") or the first-person plural ("We open our eyes") but instead she wrote it in the second person: "You open your eyes." The use of *you* gives this passage tremendous voice—this author seems to be speaking directly to me.

The first reading is just the beginning. As a writer, you need to read and reread, so you can switch your focus from what the piece is about to how she wrote this. The rereading is when you really start digging into the author's craft.

If you want to improve your writing, you have to apprentice yourself to the best writers you can find—writers you can learn from. In the chapters that follow, we're going to look at all kinds of writing, published and unpublished. I hope you will visit your library or bookstore so you can get your hands on the books I mention. We're going to take apart the writing to see what we can learn from it. How much you get out of this book will depend on how much you can read like a writer.

Don't be surprised if this kind of reading feels new and awkward at first. It may be a kind of reading you've never done before. Then again, you may not respond to a piece of writing in the same way I do. That's okay.

Writing is not an exact science. Each of us will learn something different from the same piece of writing.

Reading like a writer is like watching a magic act. The magician cuts a rope into three pieces, puts it into a hat, waves the wand, and pulls it out: Presto! The rope is back in one piece!

Our first reaction to a magic trick is: "Whoa! Awesome!" But that is quickly followed by a second reaction: "How did he *do* that?" And a split second later there is usually a third reaction: "Do it again so I can figure out how to do it myself."

I challenge you to start reading like a writer. Read once to get a full dose of the magic. But don't stop there. It's even more important to *reread* the writing to figure out how the author managed to pull off the effect. Reread it so you can start learning how to create your own kind of writing magic.

3

BUILDING CHARACTER

Characters are the most important part of a story. You can take away the setting, skim off the details, even remove all the descriptive passages until the writing is flat and ordinary, and you've still got a story. But characters are one element of writing you can't live without.

Think about Gilly Hopkins, Matilda, Maniac McGee. Think about Buck in *Call of the Wild* or Wilbur in *Charlotte's Web*. Take away these characters and you've got nothing more than a bunch of words.

Certain skills are easy to master. Once you know how to ride a bike you will always know how to do it. You'll always be able to read once you've cracked the code. But certain writing skills (like creating believable characters) take much longer to master. As a young writer, you can study how other writers create their characters, and you can experiment with different ways of doing it in your own writing.

People talk about the characters and the plot as if they are completely separate from each other. Characters and plot are deeply connected. Remember that the plot should grow out of the characters, not the other way around. My novel *Flying Solo* is about a group of sixth graders who decide to run the class when no teacher shows up. This general idea was just the shell of the story. The real story would not be what would happen *to* these kids as much as what would happen *between* them. Which students band together? Which ones would argue or get left out? I kept envisioning the different personalities to figure out what the book would be about.

If your characters are going to come alive on the page they must first come alive in your mind. This may seem strange, but that's the way a writer's imagination works. You've got to start envisioning them—faces, quirks, fears—in order for them to become real. This is a job you need to take seriously: no one on earth will know your characters better than you. While there is no one way to build a character, here are some suggestions for breathing life into your characters:

Start with what you know. Build your characters from the familiar people and animals you encounter in your life. The characters in my books tend to be like the people I know: regular folks capable of good and evil, bravery and cowardice. I don't know any superheroes or (fortunately) ax murderers, but that's okay. I'm interested in ordinary characters, and that's important. I'm going to be spending lots of time writing about them, so they have to intrigue me enough to keep me going.

I get ideas for characters by keeping my eyes open wherever I am. Once in a first grade classroom I met a very shy, very quiet girl with curly hair.

"She doesn't talk," the teacher explained to me. "She *can* talk, but she chooses not to. She's a selective mute. She's going through some kind of emotional trauma."

Those words fascinated me: *selective mute*. For a long time I wondered about that girl. What could have happened to her that had made her stop talking? I knew that someday I would return to this idea, and I did. In *Flying Solo*, the main character (Rachel White) is a selective mute.

In one town I lived in I often saw a man about my age walking three dogs. I saw him almost every day. Shirtless, he'd walk down the street, reading the newspaper, while his dogs trotted happily along behind him. In my mind I named him the Walker, and I wondered about him. Who was he? What was he doing? What was the rest of his life like? Though I have not yet written about him, the Walker is exactly the kind of character who might one day appear in one of my poems or novels.

Give physical descriptions of your characters. Kate Hallinan, an Ohio fourth grader, wrote a picture book about her dog, Ginger. She starts with a dramatic lead but doesn't rush ahead into the action. Instead she pauses on the second page to give us a mind picture of what Ginger looks like:

[Page 1:] "No, Mom!" I cried as she told me we were going to have to give Ginger away. I cried and cried. It seemed like a storm that would never end.
[Page 2:] My dog, Ginger, is a Golden Retriever, but not the color of any old Golden Retriever. She was the color of autumn, a brown, golden, yellow, orange sort of color, but not just the color was different. *She* was different. She was different, and she was my dog.

Use all five senses when you describe a character. In *Yolanda's Genius* by Carol Fenner, Yolanda's favorite relative is Aunt Tiny, a woman so enormous she needs two seats at an outdoor concert. Look at how many different kinds of sensory details Carol Fenner uses in this wonderful description of Aunt Tiny:

> Aunt Tiny had a laugh as rich and flaky as biscuits and gravy. She wore gorgeous clothes—reds so bright and whites so pure and spanking clean. She would fix ribs, baking them slow in the oven, and serve them with red beans and steaming rice. She cooked the beans slow, too, with giant slabs of clove-studded onion.
>
> Tiny's hands were pretty as Momma's, only her nails were very long, squared-off at the tips, and polished a shiny red. She ate with delicate bites, nibbling daintily, mincing her way through rib after rib, wiping her mouth with her napkin, not getting any of the barbecue sauce on her blindingly white slacks. She smelled wonderfully of perfume and food. When she surrounded Yolanda in a big, soft hug, Yolanda could have stayed there forever, inhaling Aunt Tiny's sweetness.

Get your characters moving. Watch people. You can tell worlds about them by studying their gestures and movements. I recently observed some sixth graders coming into a classroom. One girl entered with perfect posture, marching crisply to her desk. She sat down quietly and took out her notebook. Behind her, a boy shuffled in, dragging his feet, actually kicking his backpack into the room. He reached his desk, flopped down, and drew the hood of his sweatshirt tight around his head until his face was invisible.

As a writer, you must be sure to tell not just what's happening *to* a character but what's happening *inside* that character. What is she elated about? What has him fuming with rage? That's why describing motion and gesture are such helpful tools for a writer. If you can describe those movements well enough, you give the reader a real window into that character's emotional state.

Leslie Gaillard, a fifth grader, describes her sister in a picture book she has written:

I turned on the TV to channel 22. I got up to go to the bathroom.

When I came back, just as I was ready to plop back into my seat, guess who was there? The Princess of the house. (It says so on her bedroom door.) In one hand was the TV clicker. She was flipping through the channels.

In the other hand was the glass of orange juice she was sipping so delicately. Covering her was a warm blanket made out of yarn. On her lap was a toasted bagel, and on top of the coffee table were her big, fat and ugly feet, her dainty toes wiggling with delight.

Can't you just picture Leslie's sister's annoying little self? In this passage the girl's movements come alive through carefully chosen details—''*flipping* through the channels,'' the ''dainty toes *wiggling* with delight.''

The characters we've talked about so far have all been people, but they don't have to be. In this story Eric Weeks, a sixth grader, writes about the antics of his dog Sam:

When Sam has an encounter with the vacuum, he tries to fight it like it's another dog. Whenever it comes real close to him he does something between a bark and a yelp. He tries to bite the vacuum, but he just takes a nip since it's hard and made of plastic and he can't penetrate his teeth into it at all.

Get your characters talking. We reveal ourselves by what comes out of our mouths—not just what we say but how we say it. You can get your characters talking in a dramatic scene. Dialogue is a wonderful tool, but be careful it doesn't take over. Put in too much dialogue and your text begins to sound like a play. Writers choose carefully where and when to include conversation between characters.

In *Flying Solo,* Rachel stopped talking earlier in the school year when a classmate, a boy who had a crush on her, died suddenly in his sleep. Rachel sometimes writes notes for her friend Missy to read aloud. In this scene Rachel uses notes to confront Bastian, a boy who used to tease Tommy Feathers when he was alive:

"You raced him to the bus," Missy read in an angry voice, "but as soon as he started you'd stop and let him keep running all the way to the bus. He was a slow kid and you teased him. You called him Doctor Drool."

"So what?" Bastian said, shrugging. "Is it my fault the kid drooled? Yeah, I teased him. I tease everybody. Name one person in here I *don't* tease, huh?"

Nobody spoke.

"What?" Bastian shouted. "You think I was the only one, huh?"

"Shush!" Karen said.

"Hey, I didn't kill him!" Bastian hissed. His eyes narrowed. His voice got low and gravelly. "The kid had medical problems, okay? He died in his sleep! And he was a pain in the butt! Everybody's afraid to say it, but it's true! You know it and I know it!"

21

"Quiet!" Jasmine warned, but Rachel was writing again, lips compressed with fury.

"I think we should stop—" Jessica began.

"Yeah, maybe we'd better—"

"You should talk!" Bastian shouted at Rachel. "You were the one he called his sweetheart, remember? Why don't you write about the fifty million hearts and Valentines he made you!"

"Will you please keep it down!" Karen begged but Bastian ignored her.

"Remember that time he asked you to be his girlfriend?" he yelled at Rachel. "You blew him off! You just laughed at him! SHUT UP, RACHEL! JUST SHUT UP!"

One important tip about dialogue is be careful not to include too much dialogue in which nothing happens, as exemplified below:

"Hello," I said.

"Hi, it's me."

"Oh, what's up?"

"Oh, not much. Whatcha doin'?"

"Talking to you."

If dialogue goes on too long it can bore your reader. When you write dialogue, make sure you cut to the meat of what's going on. The dialogue should in some way move the action of the story forward. If it doesn't, cut it.

When you think of dialogue, don't limit yourself to what gets spoken out loud. You can also use inner dialogue to reveal the flow of mental talk in a character's head. Inner dialogue is a great way to flesh out a character, as in this scene of mine about a boy at bat:

I stood in the batting box, spit twice, planted my feet. "No batter, no batter," the catcher said, but I ignored him and glared out at the pitcher. My heart was racing. I took a few practice swings, pointing the barrel of the bat straight at the pitcher. Take it easy, I told myself. Don't forget to breathe. And don't go fishing. Make him throw strikes. Wait for your pitch.

Beware "good guys" and "bad guys." Don't make good characters too good, or bad characters too bad. Otherwise your characters will come across as two-dimensional. In real life people generally have a mix of both qualities. You'll make your bad characters more believably evil if you at least mention some of their human qualities. And your heroes will be more realistic if you include a few of their flaws and failings.

The challenge for a writer is to reveal the complexity of human nature. I like to explore contradictions in the people I write about: for example, an altar boy who plays vicious defensive end on the football team. Showing the human contradictions helps bring a character alive as a real person with many different sides.

My mother, for instance, is about as antiwar as you can get. She was one of those people who marched against the Vietnam War. But many times I'd catch her, late at night, watching war movies. A contradiction such as this one gives a character life and makes her more interesting. And it offers interesting possibilities in developing the action of your story.

You should also be cautious about having one of your characters change too suddenly during the course of the story. In *Spider Boy,* Bobby Ballenger is taunted by Chick Hall, the class bully. This continues for weeks until Chick Hall finally does something awful to Bobby. In an early draft, I wrote a scene in which Chick sincerely apologizes to Bobby for what he has done. But when I reread that scene it didn't sound right. Chick is both cocky and mean, and it didn't ring true that he would suddenly change from Mr. Despicable to Mr. Nice. In real life, people rarely change like that. In the end, I decided to cut that scene and leave Chick the way he was.

Two more tips regarding character:

Name your characters. The simple act of giving a name for a character can make that character real, both for your and for the reader. You'll want to select a name or nickname that suggests the character's personality. If I'm writing about a man who plays practical jokes and causes trouble, for example, I'll try to choose a nickname such as Rowdy to suggest his mischievousness.

Don't try to juggle too many characters in one piece of writing. Too many characters can confuse the reader. I should know. I grew up as the oldest of nine kids. When I wrote *Fig Pudding* I couldn't imagine how I could possibly handle so many kids in the book. So I did something my parents could never do: I cut the family down to six kids.

The sixth grade class in *Flying Solo* contains eighteen kids. I knew it would be difficult to juggle so many characters, so I decided that most of the kids would be background characters. They would have few lines and very little impact on the story. Only five or six of the kids stand out as main characters. That made the book much easier to write.

Some writers create their characters in one swift motion, through a leap of the imagination. Others take more time to get to know their characters. Author Carolyn Coman says that for her, creating a new character is like getting to know a new person. As you will see in the next chapter, she finds it helpful to actually write letters to her characters! Though I don't do this, I do spend lots of time thinking about my characters, hearing them talk to each other. There's no one recipe for making your characters come alive. As a writer, you will have to experiment to find what works best for you.

THOUGHTS ON CREATING CHARACTERS

by Carolyn Coman

Carolyn Coman is one of my favorite writers. Her first young adult novel, Tell Me Everything, *was followed by* What Jamie Saw, *which was named a Newbery Honor Book, an award that goes to the best fiction for young readers every year.*

Carolyn Coman's books are intense, realistic, sometimes painful, filled with unforgettable characters. The slow process she uses to get to know her characters is fascinating. She carries on a kind of mental dialogue between herself and the people who will become part of her books. I'm struck by the deep respect Carolyn has for her characters.

I don't create characters so much as I make room inside my mind and heart for them to come and get me. I am drawn to characters who make me feel deeply—make me mad, confuse me, make me wonder, break my heart, stagger me with what they are up against.

My characters must fundamentally interest me, and they must have room to grow. I spend a lot of time with them over the course of writing a story, thinking and wondering about them, figuring out who they are and what has happened in their lives, observing them closely. When they are finally willing to speak to me, I listen carefully to the sounds of their voices and to what they are trying to say.

Some characters appear strong and clear almost from the beginning, yakking away, doing things, asserting themselves into a story. Others hold back, ghost-like, for so long that I despair of ever getting to know them inside out.

Sometimes a character comes to me out of nowhere, and I have to go looking for the story of what happens to him or her. Sometimes the story idea comes first and I have to wait and see what characters are needed to play it out. As long as I have something to start with, even a crumb of an idea, I'm grateful, and go from there.

The journey I make in getting to know, understand, and love a character is much like the journey I make in getting to know anyone I love—one that is made over time, day by day, sharing experiences (some of which become the plot of the book), observing, learning when to take the lead and when to sit still and wait and see what happens all on its own.

When I am first getting to know a character, I often experience a deep shyness. Who is this person and how dare I be writing about someone I don't even know? It seems the height of presumption, and I usually beg pardon from the character (who doesn't even have a name yet, or has a name that will change as the story develops). I stick with whoever is emerging, though, and eventually the shyness evaporates.

I think about my characters the way I think about my friends and family and people I read about in the newspaper. I wonder about them, daydream about them, worry about their situations, talk to them, try to get them to open up to me.

In trying to know and see them clearly, I write about them separate from the story itself. I write directly to them, asking them questions, telling them what I am dying to know about them. (I ask a lot of questions, period. My journal is filled with questions to myself as the writer, to my characters, about the story. Everything starts with questions.) I talk about them with my friends; if I'm lucky I have some dreams about them; I imagine what they look like; I look for pictures and people who remind me of them. I make note of expressions they use, the particular way they have of speaking, their gestures, their tics. I try not to get impatient (with them or myself) when I don't understand them right away, or can't figure out what happens next, or can't hear their voices.

It's funny to think that much of this whole complicated process takes place inside my mind. No wonder I am such a daydreamer.

While each character is becoming who he or she is, I borrow a million little traits and tics and stories and physical attributes that I have observed and stored away over the course of my life. My character may look like someone I know, may be a combination of different personality traits I find interesting, may talk like a member of my own family, but ultimately the character is his or her own person, unique the way each and every one of us is.

My characters must stand on their own, and I must stand by them. Respect for them is essential, as it is in all aspects of writing. As with the people in my life, some characters are easier to know and love than others. It's necessary for me to love them, because as a writer I am often called upon to look at them and say hard things. And the only way to do that without being cruel or disdainful is to have an understanding of and compassion for the wide range of what it means to be a human being.

When a character finally comes alive, into his or her own, with a particular voice and manner and take on the world, it's cause for celebration, a real gift. That's when characters can really surprise you, when you discover things about them that you hadn't suspected—a sense of humor, an optimism, a passion for fishing—*when* the story itself can take an interesting turn. Once the characters are fully formed, I feel that they work with me to tell the story the way it needs to be told. At that point my work becomes more listening and recording than dreaming up possibilities. What an amazing process it all is—a bit of a miracle, definitely a mystery.

VOICE: CONNECTING WITH THE READER

Not too long ago I received a large envelope containing letters from a class of students who had read some of my books. I enjoyed all the letters, but one really stood out:

Dear Mr. Ralph Fletcher,

Hi. My name is Andy Schlaack, and I like toaster ovens (really, I do!), but that's not why I'm writing. I'm writing about two of your books. Mrs. Spryou, my teacher, just finished reading Fig Pudding *by you. It was splendifurous (that's a made-up word. Don't look it up.), and it was sad when Brad died. Hey! I forgot to tell you when it was splendifurous*

*(remember, made-up word). Well, that was near
the end when Josh stepped in the fig pudding and
Uncle Eddie ate it without knowing Josh had
stepped in it. We've also been reading* A Writer's
Notebook *by you. I liked the stories and tips. Well,
it's been swell. Y'all come back now, y'hear?*

> *Your reader and friend,*
> *Andy "SCH" Schlaack*

PS Write back if you want.

This letter made me laugh out loud. I gave it to my
wife and kids so they could read it. I enjoyed the humor,
the wisecracking asides, the odd details (toaster ovens?),
and that made-up word. But more than anything I enjoyed the voice of the author. It came through loud and
clear. How could I *not* reply to a letter like that?

In the last chapter we looked at different ways to
breathe life into your characters. But you must not forget
the most important character: the narrator. If your narrator sounds dull and colorless, the reader won't follow
you very far into the writing. As a writer you've got to
give the narrator a compelling voice.

Voice in writing sounds like a mysterious word, but
it really isn't hard to understand. When I talk about
voice in writing, all I mean is the sense of the author's
personality that comes through the words on the paper.
Writing with voice sounds honest and authentic. It has

conviction and integrity. It has the quirks and rhythms of human speech. Writing with voice makes us feel as if we're listening to a real person. Many writers sound perfectly natural when they talk, but somehow their words get all stiff and formal when they're written down. In this chapter we'll look at different ways you can breathe voice into your writing.

Think of writing as chatting on paper. As you write, imagine yourself on the morning after a sleepover with your best friend. You're sitting in the kitchen, eating cereal or bagels, chatting away. Be yourself. Try to get that easy tone—comfortable and conversational— into the words you put to paper.

In *Mick Harte Was Here* by Barbara Park, the narrator is Phoebe, the sister of a boy who got killed in a bicycle accident. On the very first page of the book, the author establishes Phoebe's voice. It is the natural voice of an ordinary kid, and you'll notice that she often begins sentences with *like* and *and*. This makes her sound real:

> Just let me say right off the bat, it was a bike accident.
> It was about as "accidental" as you can get, too.
> Like Mick wasn't riding crazy. Or dodging in and out of traffic. And both his hands were on the handlebars and all like that.

His tire just hit a rock. And he skidded into the back of a passing truck. And that was that. There wasn't a scratch on him. It was a head injury. Period.

In *Slam!* author Walter Dean Myers also establishes the distinct voice of the narrator in the very first paragraph of his novel:

Basketball is my thing. I can hoop. Case closed. I'm six four and I got the moves, the eye, and the heart. You can take my game to the bank and wait around for the interest. With me it's not like playing a game, it's like the only time I'm being real. Bringing the ball down the court makes me feel like a bird that just learned to fly. I see guys moving down in front of me and everything feels and looks right. Patterns come up and a small buzz comes into my head that starts to build up and I know it won't end until the ball swishes through the net. If somebody starts messing with my game it's like they're getting into my head. But if I've got the ball it's okay, because I can take care of the situation. That's the word and I know it the same way I know my tag, Slam. Yeah, that's it. Slam. But without the ball, without the floorboards under my feet, without the mid-court line that takes me halfway home, you can get to me.

Notice not only what the author is writing about (basketball) but how he makes Slam's voice seem so real. When I reread this passage, I noticed a couple of things. First, he uses conversational slang that has the authentic ring of the inner city: "I can hoop" and "messing with my game." He also alternates long sentences with short sentences that are really sentence fragments: "Case closed." This, too, has the sound of human speech. Listen to people talking and you'll notice that they rarely speak in complete, grammatically correct sentences.

Follow your passions. There's something else going on in the beginning of *Slam!* We can tell immediately that the narrator is talking about something he's passionate about. That's an important source of voice in writing: passion. Writing with voice carries honesty and conviction. If you're anything like me, you write with the most voice when you're writing about something you care a lot about.

Let me tell you a quick story about Dylan Jacobsen. I met him when I visited his school on Long Island, New York. He was an eighth grader, a tall kid who sat in the back of the class, and he ran his mouth the whole time I was there. Trouble with a capital T. Ignoring him, I asked the kids in class to make an "Expert List," a list of topics they knew a lot about. When I strolled over to Dylan's desk I saw the following list:

1. Girls
2. Guns
3. Surfing

"Do you really know a lot about surfing?" I asked.
"Oh, yeah," he said, smirking at the boy beside him.
"Like what?" I asked. "Tell me."
And he did. He told me about the first time he ever went surfing. He told me about different kinds of surfboards. He explained to me what it's like to go out when the surf is high after a storm. He told me what it's like to be inside the curl of the wave. Pretty soon he wasn't smirking anymore. As he talked he got more and more excited. He started explaining to me all the different injuries you can get while surfing.

"Whoa," I said. "You know a ton about this stuff, you know that? Why don't you write about it?"

Dylan glared at me, shrugged, then bent to his task. He started to write. Here's the beginning of what he wrote:

I got my first surf board for my eleventh birthday and I've been surfing ever since. Watch me on the beach with my board and my wet suit. You probably figure I'm checking out the girls (you're right— I am) but I'm also scoping out the swell. The waves. You don't mess with the surf, especially around here. In school if you read a problem wrong on a test, hey, no big deal, but if you read the surf wrong and it mashes you against a rock or jetty somewhere, well, you will be one hurting puppy, I guarantee you that.

Dylan's piece crackles with energy, juice, voice, because he found something that really mattered to him. Dylan loved surfing, and you can feel his passion from the way he writes about it.

Think audience. When my writing lacks voice, I ask myself: Who do I want to read this? Who am I writing this for, anyway?

James Stevenson's picture book *I Meant to Tell You* chronicles some special times he shared with his daughter. It's a simple book but it really touches me, maybe because I have my own small children. The book begins: "I meant to tell you, before I forget: I remember when you were small." Right away we know that the narrator is speaking to his child. In these simple words you can hear the unmistakable voice of a parent: strong, tender, full of love.

If your writing seems flat and voiceless, you might try writing it first as a letter to someone. Letter writing tends to be full of voice because we know there is a sympathetic audience to read our words.

In *Letters from a Slave Girl,* Mary E. Lyons tells the story through a series of letters written by Harriet Jacobs. Harriet's mother and father die when she is a child, but she writes many letters to them. You'll notice that these letters contain spelling mistakes, since they are written by a girl who never had the chance to go to school. Still, the author's voice is unmistakable:

24 December, 1826

Dear Daddy,

    Christmas week dont seem the same with out you to bring us wooden pull-toys and a wild duck for Christmas supper. When you went away lass spring, me and John was left to the mursey of this wurld. John say Slavery made you sicken and die. When you couldn't save money for freedom, he say, you felt like a possum trapped in a tree. He is not over it yet.

Be honest with the reader. Be honest when you write. That's so easy to say and so hard to do. Being honest with the reader requires that you first be honest with yourself. In the following piece, sixth grader Katie Lathrop reflects on her parents.

First Thoughts

I love my mom. This morning she dropped me off at the bus stop and said: "Aren't you going to give me a kiss?"

I said, "No, I don't have time!" and shut the car door. I knew the minute I said "NO!" I would regret it. The whole day I have been thinking about me not giving my mom a kiss.

Why are kids at this age like this? Is it because we want our independence? When you are young your parents are the best thing in the world. Then they become stupid and don't know anything when you are a teen. Then when you get to be an adult they are brilliant.

I don't know why we are like this. I know deep down inside of me that my mom is one of my best friends. She will sit and talk with me about things that are important to me. Sometimes we will just sit and laugh.

Katie's writing contains some sarcastic humor along with a convincing, soul-searching honesty. I connect with the kind of writing where it feels as if the author is being honest.

Experiment with different kinds of voice. Not all audiences are the same. Most of us learn at an early age that talking with a friend is quite different from talking to an adult, teacher, policeman, or storekeeper. In the same way, a writer doesn't always use the same voice for every kind of writing. You may use a more casual voice in fiction than you would use when applying for a job or writing a complaint letter to a local restaurant. As you can see from the following example, there will be times when you deliberately choose to use a more formal voice in a piece of writing.

We have a basic rule in our family: our kids can't spend money if they don't have it. They can't buy things from each other using a promise to pay at some later date. Our two oldest kids, Taylor and Adam, were well aware of this rule. But Taylor (seventh grade) wanted to sell some Magic cards to Adam (fourth grade), and Adam wanted to buy them. Taylor came up with the idea of writing a contract. This writing serves its purpose well partly because it uses a kind of legal voice that gives it seriousness and authority.

This contract hereby pronounces that Adam Curtis must give Taylor Curtis any money he gets as soon as possible until he has given him a total of $40.00 (forty dollars). During this time, Adam Curtis may use Taylor Curtis' 60 card green deck whenever he chooses. Once Taylor Curtis has accumulated 40 dollars from Adam Curtis, Adam Curtis shall thereby assume full ownership of the green deck, except but one card, Force of Nature. Adam and Taylor must have full approval of their parents to sign this contract. However, once permission has been granted, the parents of the aforementioned individuals may not take back the permission which had been already granted (they can't change their minds). Once Taylor and Adam have signed this contract, they are unable to take it back. If at any time Adam Curtis decides not to pay the money his access to the deck is discontinued and any money he has given Taylor Curtis is not returned.

Your writing voice is like a handshake; it makes the connection with the reader. For this reason it is a crucial ingredient in any piece of writing. As a writer you can use humor, sarcasm, little asides to make your narrator sound like a real person. It's worth the effort. When writing has that authentic a-real-person-is-saying-something-important-to-me quality, it's hard to put down.

Look at the following story written by Gina Pedone, a New York fifth grader:

When my brother was born, he wasn't exactly a bouncing baby boy. He had a lot of problems with his insides and, well, I just couldn't understand it then. I was still waiting for my teeth to come out for the tooth fairy to come.

A lot of times Mom would stay at the hospital helping the nurse care for the sick child. Back then I didn't know what was happening and I got jealous. He got cared for 24 hours a day and I got stuck with next-door neighbors who tried feeding me orange marmalade sandwiches almost every day.

After five operations the doctors said he was well enough to come home. Just to look at him would bring tears to your eyes. He was always pale and had to be fed through a tube from inside his stomach. A lot of times he would pull out the tube and we would have to rush him to the hospital so it could be put back in. It was horrible.

After a few more operations the tube went away and he was beginning to look normal. Today he still goes for check-ups, and he does have epilepsy, but he is a regular, annoying, bratty younger sibling. Thank God he is!

THOUGHTS ON VOICE

by Han Nolan

Han Nolan is a terrific writer. She has written three novels: If I Should Die Before I Wake, Send Me Down a Miracle, *and* Dancing on the Edge. Dancing on the Edge *won the National Book Award in 1997. Han Nolan's books are filled with power, magic, and voice. In the following pages, Han Nolan explains how you can breathe voice into your writing.*

Do you like to wear shoes or go barefoot? Do you like to sit in the back of the classroom or up front, or maybe somewhere in the middle? Do you wear your hair short or long? Do you like having lots and lots of friends, or just one or two special friends? What's your favorite food? What's your favorite sport? Do you even like sports?

All of your answers to questions like these help you to know what kind of person you are. Of course you know everybody is different. Even if you and your best friend both wear the same style of jeans and matching T-shirts, and both love potato chips and funny movies, you still will find that there are things about you that make you different from each other, things that make you special. You might say that all these likes and dislikes, the way you do things you do, give you your own personal style. Maybe you didn't know you had style. Maybe you thought fashion models and athletes and actors were the only people with style, but we all have style.

We also have style as writers, whether you like to write mystery stories or science fiction, romance or poetry. Each writer has a style, or what we call a voice. A writer's voice is unique as his or her own fingerprints.

Let's say you and your best friend both write a mystery story about a haunted house. Both stories have ghosts and both stories have the same characters in it, Mike and Lisa. Will the story sound the same? Of course not, because each of you will tell your story your own way. You will each choose your own set of words to tell the story and your own sentence structure. So your best friend's story might have lots of short sentences and exclamations, and your story might have longer sentences with lots of commas. Your friend's might be mostly narrative, while yours has mostly dialogue. There are so many ways that a story might be different, as many ways as there are people on the earth.

Many writers and editors believe that voice is the most important element a writer can develop, and editors will reject a story if they feel the story has no voice.

"Wait a minute," you might say. "How could a story not have a voice? That's like a person not having a personality, and everybody has a personality, don't they?"

We all do have a voice, just as everybody has a personality, but our true voices can get lost, exactly the same way we can lose our true personality or lose our sense of style.

I bet you know some people in your class who have decided that they don't really like who they are. One might have decided that her hair is too frizzy and another that he's too short. These people want to be anybody but themselves so they look around the class, or maybe they look at someone in a grade higher than theirs who they've decided is much cooler than they are, and they decide they're going to be just like that person. They walk, talk, dress, eat, laugh as much like that person as they can. They do a perfect imitation, but that's all it is, an imitation. All the things these people used to love, all the things that used to make them laugh, their favorite foods, their favorite sports, all of these disappear. They lose their personality and borrow someone else's.

This happens in writing, too. A writer will look at his or her writing and compare it to someone else's, and decide: "My writing looks like a baby wrote it." Or, "My writing is so stupid." Or, "My writing is too serious; I want it to be funny like hers."

Of course we all want to get better at our writing just as we all want to grow up. We can't stay exactly the same all our lives. The problem comes when we try to be other than who we really are, either in our writing or in our personalities. This happens whenever we change to please someone else, or because we are afraid of what people might think if we did it our way.

A writer who decides his writing is stupid might decide to throw in a lot of big words and string together a lot of long sentences, just so he can impress people. You know what happens then? Poof! The true voice disappears, and usually so does a good story. Or a student might write a story a certain way just to please the teacher, or just because she thinks she can get an A if she writes this way, or even to please the parent.

When we do this we have become too aware of ourselves and how we can please and impress others, and less aware of the stories we're wanting to tell. When your story comes from inside you, when it comes from your heart, or from something you care about or something you love, even if it's something like haunted houses or Martians, then you know your story will have a voice, your voice.

When you are young your writer's voice just comes naturally to you. But as you grow and change and get influenced by friends and family and people at school, that voice can start slipping away.

So how do you hold on to your true voice? How can you improve your writing style without losing that voice?

First it is important to remember why you are writing. If it isn't an assignment from a teacher, then usually you are writing because you have a story you want to tell. If you write it down and want to share it, then you have to be good at communicating just what you mean to say so the reader sees the same things you see. If you're trying to be fancy or show off or sound intelligent instead of trying to help your reader see the story just as you do, then you've lost your voice. So tell the story as clearly and cleanly and as simply as you can. Create pictures for your readers with the words you choose so the reader can see just what you see, and hear in their mind the same voices you hear in your head when you write dialogue.

Do you have a favorite author? Have you read more than one book by that author? When you do, you start to get a feel for how that author writes. You start to know their style, their voice. And if you've read a lot of books by the same author, you get to where you can tell that a page from a book someone is reading was written by your favorite author, even if it's a book you've never read. You recognize the voice. Reading several books by the same author can help you understand voice better, and just reading them can help you develop your own voice without even trying. Just read the books.

If you like stories of a certain type, like science fiction or fantasy, then read several books by many different authors but all on the same topic, and see if you can tell how their voices are different. Can you guess something about the author's personality just by reading her books? Usually you can, even if she's writing about an evil character and she is as nice as can be. You can still get hints of the author through the voice. It's like leaving fingerprints all over a glass. The author's fingerprints are all over the stories. Thinking about this while you read can help you identify different authors' voices. It can help you to improve your own voice, too.

Of course, the best way to develop and improve your voice is to write a lot, and not just stories or class assignments. The best way I know to develop your voice, especially if you feel you don't have one, is to keep a journal or a writer's notebook. This isn't the same as a diary, where you list what you did that day. A journal/notebook should be a book filled with pages and pages of paper where you can write down all your private thoughts and feelings and ideas, even if you think they're dumb or daring or scary thoughts. This is a book you will never show anyone, so you can say anything you please.

The more you write in the notebook, the more your true voice will appear, and the more you will get to know who the real you is. When you write in a notebook you can let go. You can let go of what others might think about your writing. You can let go of any worries about getting graded, and especially, you can let go of judging yourself. In a notebook, nothing is good or bad, stupid or silly. If you write honestly, your notebook will be filled with the true you. And just think: nobody can do you better than you can. Nobody can tell a story in just the way you tell it, because you're unique. You're one in a million. You've got style! You've got voice!

CONFLICT:
HERE COMES TROUBLE

In a good story something happens. A boy runs away, gets teased, falls in love. Maybe the main character has a stroke of good luck, though more likely, the luck turns bad. Trouble is a necessary ingredient to writing. Writing without trouble lacks tension.

Picture a space capsule orbiting the earth. In space it hurtles around our planet with nothing to slow it down. But as the capsule returns to earth it reenters the atmosphere and begins to strike molecules of air. This creates friction, which in turn creates a tremendous amount of heat (space capsules are designed with heat shields to protect the astronauts). The heat creates drama, danger, the possibility of death.

You can experience this right where you are sitting. Rub your hand hard on a countertop and you'll feel heat on your hand. That's why it's dangerous to scuffle on a rug—if you're not careful, you can get a burn.

What will readers feel as they move through your writing? Will there be any resistance to produce friction and heat? If not, the writing can be flat and downright boring to read, as seen in the following passage:

I took my son Robert camping. For weeks he had been begging me, and I finally carved out the time to take him. We took a two-hour drive straight north, arrived at the trailhead, put on our backpacks, and started hiking.

We started hiking through some beautiful scenery. For the first quarter mile we walked through a field of wildflowers. We stepped over lots of gurgling streams and Robert counted seven small waterfalls right beside the trail. After a while we started climbing. Soon we could look up at a green mountain decked out with wisps of clouds. I wished I had thought to bring my camera.

Are you yawning yet? Honestly now, how much more of this would you like to read? Not too much, I'll bet. This story lacks any trouble, any heat. Things are going *too* well. I know that something had better happen in this story, and happen quick, or I'm going to lose my reader.

The simplest way to create heat in a piece of writing is through *conflict*, which comes in three basic varieties:

1. PERSON AGAINST PERSON

This kind of conflict involves a struggle between strong-willed personalities. Often you have one person trying to achieve some goal (the protagonist) and another attempting to stop him or her (the antagonist). You find this kind of conflict in writing about wars, detective mysteries (detective vs. criminal), fairy tales, and many other kinds of stories.

In my novel *Spider Boy,* Bobby Ballenger moves to a new town, where he runs smack into Chick Hall. Chick makes fun of Bobby's interest in spiders. As the book continues, Chick tries harder and harder to intimidate Bobby. This puts Bobby into a situation he's never been in before.

In *War with Grandpa* by Robert Kimmel Smith, a boy gets booted out of his beloved bedroom when his grandfather moves in and takes that room. The "war" consists of situations, both humorous and serious, in which the two characters try to outfox each other.

2. PERSON AGAINST NATURE

It's scary out there, and that's why movies like *Jaws* and *Twister* are so popular, as well as survival books such as *My Side of the Mountain* by Jean Craighead George and *Hatchet* by Gary Paulsen. Readers love watching humans pit their intelligence against the brute forces of the natural world.

Dakota Dugout, a picture book by Ann Warren Turner, depicts the lives of settlers as they struggle against drought, fire, heat, and bitter cold. In the person vs. nature conflict, we see not only how characters overcome hostile forces of nature, but also what they discover about themselves in the process.

3. INTERNAL CONFLICT

Look at the first paragraph of this story by Adam Field, a seventh grader in Maine:

Which Life for Me?

All my life I've been told many things about two different people—Mom and my Dad. My mother and her relatives have had nothing but bad things to say about my father. Mom says that Dad took off the day after I was born. On the other hand, my Grammie, Dad's mother, says that Dad just wasn't ready for marriage and that he was put in a tough spot by my mother. I never knew who I should believe. Little did I know that at the age of ten I would have a chance to make my own decision.

I love psychological books, which is probably why the internal conflict is my favorite. Inner conflicts put characters into situations where they have to make tough decisions about what is right and what is wrong. This conflict requires you as a writer to delve deeply inside your characters, to closely examine their motives and impulses.

Bastian is one of the main characters in my novel *Flying Solo*. Since Bastian's father is in the Air Force, he has become accustomed to moving every year or two. He doesn't mind the fact that he and his family will be moving to Hawaii until his father tells him that his new puppy will have to be put in quarantine for four months! This information forces Bastian to do some soul-searching: is it fair to lock a puppy up like that for such a long time? What is the right thing to do? Bastian's inner torment is invisible to the other characters, but it strongly affects the way he acts throughout the book.

These three different kinds of conflict are not always distinct. Often you will find them mixed together; it's not at all unusual to see several different kinds of conflict operating in the same piece of writing.

Here are a few tips for creating lifelike conflict in your writing:

• *Don't expect readers to wait too long before finding out what the problem is.* I think of writing as a river (story) flowing over a waterfall (climax or hot spot). Don't make the mistake of starting your piece of writing too far upstream. Here's my rule of thumb: start it close enough to the waterfall so that the roar is audible from the very beginning.

• *Slow down crucial moments.* Writer Barry Lane calls this exploding a moment. I call it slowing down a hot spot. Whatever you call it, this is an excellent tool to build suspense in a piece of writing. Take the moment with the most conflict, the most tension, and write that part as a dramatic scene using details, dialogue, and a frame-by-frame slow-motion focus.

• *Don't resolve conflicts too quickly.* The great Charles Dickens once gave this advice to writers: "Make them laugh, make them weep, but above all make them wait." This is one of the ways to build the suspense in a piece of writing.

In fact, the conflict in a story usually gets worse before it gets better. Think of *Where the Wild Things Are* by Maurice Sendak, a book we all read when we were younger. Max misbehaves and gets sent to his bedroom. But the trouble gets worse: he sails off to a faraway land where he encounters ferocious monsters who threaten him.

• *Beware stories that end abruptly or too predictably.*

The conflict should get resolved in a way that's satisfying. If it feels satisfying to you as the writer, chances are pretty good it will feel that way to the reader.

Look at the first draft of a story by Melissa Baldassari, a fifth grader in New York:

My Dad

When I was about two and a half my dad always smoked. I didn't really understand why he smoked and what it meant. But sooner or later, I knew it wasn't good for him. Anyway, I didn't like the smoke in the house.

So now I did something about it. Even though my dad got mad I still did what I had to do.

"Who took my cigarettes!" my dad yelled.

"I did," said Melissa.

"AAAAAAAAA, my cigarettes all over the place!" my dad screamed fiercely. "Look what you did to my cigarettes! I don't believe this mess. Now I have to clean the mess up," my dad said, grumbling.

So every time my dad brought home cigarettes, I got into them. I just sat down and broke the cigarettes in half.

A couple months later my dad stopped smoking. Now I don't need to break cigarettes.

I'm really glad my dad stopped smoking. I hope

he doesn't smoke again. I love my dad and I will always love my dad for the rest of my life.

Melissa clearly states the conflict between herself and her father in the very first paragraph. The dramatic scene in the middle of the piece shows the conflict getting worse when she tries her way of dealing with it. But the problem gets solved very quickly when Dad just stops smoking. Notice the changes Melissa has made in her second draft:

My Dad

When I was about two and a half my dad smoked so much. I didn't really understand why he smoked and what it meant. But sooner or later, I knew it wasn't good for him. Anyway I didn't like the smoke in the house. It was like I was living in a bar. The smoke made me so sick, I couldn't take it anymore. So finally I did something about it. Even though my dad got mad, I still did what I had to do.

"Who took my cigarettes?" my dad yelled.

"I did!" I said, laughing nervously. I couldn't believe that I dared to say that!

"AAAAAAAA!" His cigarettes were all over the place. I had broken them all apart and threw them all over the floor in the living room.

"Look what you did to my cigarettes!" my dad screamed fiercely. "I don't believe this mess! Now I have to clean it up. Don't do this again or you will be punished!"

My dad always used to put me in a crib whenever I wrecked his cigarettes.

I didn't think my dad would take it that way. I didn't think that I would have gotten into trouble. All I wanted to do was make my dad stop smoking. I was afraid he would die.

So every time my dad brought home cigarettes, I got into them. I just sat down and broke the cigarettes in half.

A couple months later my dad stopped smoking.

"Melissa, guess what? I stopped smoking!"

"You said?" I said happily.

"Yes, I did, Melissa!"

"Dad, I'm glad you stopped smoking!"

"You know it's all because of you that I stopped smoking, and I'm happy that I stopped!" my dad said lovingly.

"Me too!" I said happily. Then he came over and hugged me and said, "I love you, Missy."

I'm really glad my dad stopped smoking. I hope he doesn't smoke again. I was there for my dad when he needed me, and I hope he will always be there when I need him.

This draft heightens the conflict between Melissa and her father by slowing down the action. The vivid details she adds to the first paragraph ("It was like living in a bar") intensify the narrator's anger toward her father's smoking. In the first dramatic scene Melissa adds more dialogue and more detail. This gives us a richer picture of the battle between child and parent. This draft seems more realistic to me, because the father warns he'll punish her if she breaks his cigarettes again.

In this draft Melissa had added another dramatic scene just before the end. She also alters the final paragraph. This new ending, in which she talks about the theme of love through being there for her father, gives the reader a much more satisfying resolution to the conflict.

SETTING:
THE MISSING INGREDIENT

Yo! This is the setting talking and I got a couple of complaints I want to make. Huh? I said the setting. You know: location, location, location.

Just trying to get a little attention over here. Tell you the truth, I'm getting a little tired of being ignored all the time. Why are so many writers dissing me, huh? Most times I'm totally invisible in writing—as in Missing, Absent, Gone. Folks write something, you can't tell if it's in Montana or Maui, know what I mean? Oh, yeah, sure, it's in the title maybe, but I don't want to stay

locked up in the title. I can't breathe there;
I want out. I want to shake things up. I want
to be part of the action, but I can't do a thing
unless somebody gives me a chance.

The setting has a right to complain because too often it is the missing link in writing. It's important for a writer to know a place and know it well. That's one reason I found it hard moving from New Hampshire to Alabama. New England is in my blood. After spending twenty-two years in New England I knew the seashore, the accents of the people, the Red Sox, and the Curse of the Bambino. It will take a long, long time before I can write like that about Alabama.

"A sense of place is key to all my writing," says Louise Borden, author of *The Little Ships* and *Goodbye, Charles Lindbergh*. "I think when I am writing I picture every scene in my mind and the words that come out in the writing are just describing that scene as simply and truly and clearly as I can. It is almost as if I must become the place."

Let's look at some of the ways the setting can work for you in your writing:

The setting can help you develop characters. When we think of a setting we often think of a particular place: camp, school, grandparents' house on the beach, Disney World. But the setting in a story can also focus on something quite small: a room in the attic, a hollow between bushes, the shady place behind that big rock. In the following piece James Albrecht, an Ohio sixth grader, describes a small space in his classroom:

This is so cool under here. Right now I'm under Mrs. Eggemeier's desk. Oh my God I can't think right now. My mind is going blank. Hey, I wonder what that black mark is for? I bet it was from a shoe. I wonder if Mrs. Eggemeier was the one who wrote all over her desk. Good thing there's no gum under this desk. I wonder if this wood is rotted or is it just a blackish color?

I'm struck by the chatty, conversational voice James uses to describe this place. He is bringing alive this particular place, but at the same time this description helps the reader better understand the narrator of the story.

The setting can also work as a psychological tool, helping you reveal the deepest emotions of your characters. In *Spider Boy,* Bobby Ballenger is still angry about having been forced to move from his home in Illinois to New York. I found that I could dramatize Bobby's feelings of anger and alienation by comparing where he used to live to where he lives now. In the following passage Bobby contrasts his old town in Illinois with his new home in New York:

New Paltz sure looked different from Illinois. He missed the flatness of the Midwest. It was hilly and wooded here in upstate New York, a riot of rocks, bushes, and trees. New Paltz had so many trees you only caught glimpses of the sky when you drove around. He missed riding bikes with Mike and Cody and Chad, all those afternoons when there was nothing between them and a huge dome of midwestern sky.

This passage, and others like it, helped me show how uprooted and out of place Bobby was feeling in his new home.

The setting can help you shape the plot. Characters and their habitat are linked together in many ways big and small. When you alter the place where your characters live, you fundamentally change their lives.

Think about Gary Paulsen's novel *Hatchet*. As the book begins, Brian is flying in a small plane. When it crashes Brian is thrown into the Canadian wilderness, a new setting in which he is forced to fight for his life.

The setting for most of my novel *Flying Solo* is a sixth grade classroom. Such a room is all too familiar to most of us, but this particular schoolroom is quite different in that the students are running the class without any teacher. The lack of an adult presence allows the kids to explore certain issues they had never talked about before.

The setting can help create a mood. Most writers think about the characters and plot first, the setting later (if at all). But it doesn't have to be this way. In fact, I think it's a mistake to put setting on the back burner when you write. Sometimes a particular setting and the mood it evokes can even suggest a story, as does this notebook entry by Katie Lathrop, a sixth grader:

I am sitting in my bed with the window open behind me. I can hear the cars going down the street. I hear the wind and feel it blowing on the back of my neck. It feels like I'm standing outside a house that looks empty all by myself on Halloween night. That is the feeling I get when cool wind blows on the back of my neck. Also, I hear the leaves rustling around. It is 9:59 PM and I am supposed to be asleep right now but I just had to write this because it is something to remember for a mystery story and tomorrow morning I will probably forget it. It's beginning to feel a lot like fall. My mom is coming. I have to stop writing or I'll get in trouble.

When you describe a setting you should be as specific as possible. Note that Katie doesn't just describe a place, she describes it at a particular time of day. The mood of a place is connected to the time of day: this place would feel much less eerie at noon, for example. In the same way Tim Pifer, a sixth grader, evokes a certain late-afternoon-in-winter feeling in this poem:

Winter

Crystals falling from the sky,
Kids playing on the crisp snow,
The plain trees standing as straight as statues,
The snow as bright as a fresh-bleached shirt,
Our shadows are beating us to the spot.
The shadows as black as the pit that never ends;
We have to tremble home and stand by the
   bright fire
to warm our red cold bodies.

Although I'm not a great cook, I can make a pretty mean soup. A good soup needs the freshest ingredients you can find combined with the right spices. Then it needs time to simmer in order to bring out the full flavor.

But not so fast. Often I taste the soup and realize that it still needs . . . something. Salt, maybe. Often a little bit of salt brings out the flavor.

Does your writing have something missing? Are you giving tons of information about who, what, when, and why, but no clues about the where? Do you think of setting as an afterthought—the sprinkles you put on the cake's frosting, nice but not really necessary?

Setting does matter. Stories (history) happen in a particular place. Martin Luther King, Jr., got locked in a jail in Selma, Alabama. That place will be forever linked with this event. Wilbur and Charlotte became friends in that dusty old barn. Describing the setting is more than just a necessary chore—it's a crucial element in making your writing deeper and richer.

If you're searching for a topic and drawing a blank, consider writing about a place important to you in some way. You might start by thinking about a place you know, a location that evokes memories or stirs up strong feelings. Brenda Powers, a professor and writer, suggests quickly sketching a map of the home or yard where you live or once lived. When you finish, look back over the map and ask yourself where the most potent memories seem to lie. Start digging there.

The setting doesn't have to be famous or even pleasant to be worth writing about. Zachary Reed, a seventh grader in Maine, wrote this poem about an old basketball gym:

Hardwood courts echo a mournful song
creaking out tunes of past plays

Shattering backboards faintly tingle
floor burns, fleshen imprints, torn away
An old gym, full of character
full of players who never made it
Memories of childhood reveries
last-second buzzer beaters, nylon
Everything, all intertwining, meshing
running together like watercolors
A Van Gogh of games in a swirl
swift brush strokes reveal dunks
Great players who never were
all play here, revolving around a sphere
The spirits of all who've ever played
basketballs fill their heart and sole
This old gym whispers tales of triumph
glory days waft among the sullen rafters
All the might-have-beens, almosts, so-closes
creep out from the sagging floorboards
It's memories like these that keep the game vital
they make it fantastic, they make a fanatic
In a glum gym, deprived of light
dreams of championship bloom

IT'S ABOUT TIME

Time is a funny thing. We know that time gets divided up evenly from day to day, week to week, but it sure doesn't feel that way. Certain dull days feel like they last for at least a hundred years. But there are other times when a whole weekend can get packed with so much fun it just seems to fly by.

In real life you can't speed up the clock or slow it down. But in writing you control the element of time in the same way that you control the lead, ending, main characters, setting, or plot.

One way to picture time in writing is by comparing it with filming an event on your camcorder and letting your friends watch it on the VCR. Your audience will quickly get restless if you make them sit through the whole tape. You can make the viewing experience much more enjoyable if you pick up the remote control. Then you can fast-forward through the boring stuff or rewind and replay the most exciting part so everyone can watch it again, perhaps in slow motion.

It's important to realize that real time is not the same thing as writing time. Good writers don't just sit back and let the tape run. When you write you need to be actively involved in cutting, editing, reordering, and slowing down. Let's take a look at four different ways you can control time in your writing:

1. CUTTING

Cutting may seem like a destructive thing to do to your writing, but it's not. In a way, writing is like growing rosebushes. The writing (or rosebush) usually ends up being stronger and healthier after you give it a vigorous pruning.

Let's say you want to write about a vacation your family took to Disney World. You begin by writing about packing, going to the airport, boarding the airplane. You use up so much energy writing about the trip to Florida that when you reach the part in the story where you're actually at Disney World, you discover that you've run out of gas.

As a writer you have to ask yourself: Is this what my story is really about? Is this part of the story really important? If not, don't hesitate to take it out. Cut! Delete!

70

Many writers waste too much time carefully describing a part of the story the reader really doesn't need to know about. Your story might work better if you begin with the moment when you heard the exciting news about a Disney vacation. After that you can simply skip a line and begin: "Two weeks later my family and I were standing in a drenching rain outside Epcot Center." The reader doesn't need to know all the details of how you got to Orlando or exactly what you ate during the flight. You can go directly to the actual vacation.

It's not always easy to know which parts to cut. Some writers find that they first have to write the section. Later they reread, realize it's not needed, and cut it out. Other writers mentally do the cutting as they brainstorm and prepare to write. You'll have to find which way works best for you.

Cutting allows you to skip ahead in time. When you do that you'll want to choose just the right transition word or phrase—*later, finally, the next morning, the following week*—to help the reader make a smooth transition from here to where you want them to be.

2. FOCUSING ON A NARROW SLICE OF TIME

"The secret wish of poetry is to stop time," Charles Simic says. Poems try to freeze a moment, but you could say the same about other kinds of writing, too.

When it comes to time, many writers bite off more

than they can chew. They make the mistake of trying to describe every inning of the baseball game, every ride at the amusement park, every hour of the field trip, every animal at the zoo. As a result, the writing ends up sounding like what it is—a list.

When I write I always ask myself: How might I narrow the time frame of my story? I could write all about visiting with my grandmother, but what would happen if I decided instead to focus on the time we spent baking bread? I could have written all about the first time I had to baby-sit an eighteen-month-old baby, but the writing came out much better when I focused on describing what it was like the first time I changed his diaper. Narrowing the time frame often makes the writing sound more dramatic and immediate.

3. SLOWING DOWN THE HOT SPOT

Many writers have wonderful moments in their writing, but they rush through them. I think that's a big mistake. Readers don't want to skip quickly through the crucial sad, scary, exciting, or touching parts. If you create an important moment, slow it down. Create a space in your writing so the reader can linger and see exactly what's going on. Slowing down the hot spot is an excellent way to make the reader feel like part of the action.

Let me share an excerpt from a story I'm working on:

Member of the Family

We had been waiting for this moment for a long time. It had taken over a year to adopt a boy from China, but the day was finally here. The whole family had been up since 7 A.M., even though the plane from China wasn't scheduled to arrive until 3 P.M. At the airport my sister and I sat on the floor by the gate, playing Fish or War, reading books, eating Nerds.

"When is he going to be here?" my sister asked for the one millionth time.

I held up three fingers.

"It's already past three," she hissed until Dad and Mom told her to shush. They both looked a little nervous. They had read the newspaper, drunk their coffee, and checked over all the official adoption papers at least twenty times to make sure everything was in order.

"There it is," Mom said, pointing at the runway. In seconds we all had our faces pushed against the glass, watching the big jet taxi toward us. Finally it parked by our gate.

"Well, this is it," Dad said. "Let's not overwhelm him. He's bound to be shy."

At that moment the door to the plane opened.

"He'll probably come out last," Mom whispered.

But the first thing we saw was a tall flight attendant woman holding hands with a little Chinese boy. He looked scared. For a second we were all quiet, but Dad stepped right up and walked toward him.

"Mr. Walters?" the stewardess asked, but Dad totally ignored her.

"Honien?" Dad asked. He knelt on the maroon carpet so his head was about even with Honien's. The boy was wearing a black turtleneck shirt, blue shorts, and rainbow suspenders to hold them up. I could see that he was holding a picture—a photo of us! He kept looking at the picture and staring at Dad. My sister giggled. Honien bit his lower lip. He looked so adorable and so serious!

"Here," Dad whispered. He held out a little yellow truck. When Honien didn't take it, Dad started to slowly drive the truck up the boy's belly. Honien smiled at that, so Dad drove the truck all the way up his chest, across his shoulders, and up the back of his head. Honien started to giggle. He took the yellow truck.

"That's for you, my little boy!" Dad whispered. He tickled Honien, and the boy fell onto the carpet. When Dad tickled him some more, Honien started to laugh really loud. People were watching, but Dad didn't seem to care. He tickled Honien and the whole time he kept saying: "My little boy! My little boy!" over and over and over.

In this story I tried to slow the hot spot in several ways:

1. Dialogue to give the scene immediacy
2. Thoughts and feelings—not just what's happening *to* the characters but what's happening *inside* them
3. Small details—the maroon carpet, the rainbow suspenders, the yellow truck—to slow the reader's focus
4. Frame-by-frame slow motion describing the movements of the characters

Remember: slow motion is a dramatic way to freeze a crucial moment in a film, but a movie shot entirely in slow motion would quickly become tedious. Slowing the hot spot will create drama in your writing, but you need to choose the right time to use this technique and to be careful you don't overdo it.

4. USING FLASHBACK

When you write, you may feel limited by having to write about what the character is doing at that particular time. Flashback allows you to break out of any given moment, and let a character relive an important event that happened in the past.

It's difficult to think of a book that does *not* include the use of flashback. You may remember the moment early in *Hatchet* when Brian thinks back on the Secret—

the moment when he saw his mother in a car with a strange man.

Often a writer will describe some object, event, or sensory detail that triggers the flashback. Halfway through my novel *Flying Solo* Rachel White is standing outside during recess. In this scene the smell of the rain triggers a flashback about her father:

> Rachel stood on the playground watching the other kids. She heard a plane in the distance. The air smelled like rain.
>
> She thought of her father.
>
> The rain smell reminded her of one summer day he took her to the playground. It started pouring rain but they didn't leave. Instead, they stayed on the swings, singing at the top of their lungs while their clothes got soaked.

Flashback lets you give readers important information about the past experiences (triumphs or humiliations) that have shaped a character. And it allows you to give a sense of a character's inner life by revealing what memories haunt that person's consciousness.

Be selective when you write a flashback. Writers don't just pick any old event from a character's past. You'll want to carefully choose a memory that helps reveal what makes that character tick.

Try to be aware of time in your writing, and never forget that when you create a piece of writing you control the remote control. You can hit the buttons for rewind (flashback), fast forward (skip ahead), delete (cut), or slow motion (for slowing down the hot spot). The skillful use of time is one of the best ways I know to make your writing come alive.

The following story was written by Noelle Parris, a third grader in New York City. I admire several things about Noelle's story—the voice, the wonderful details—but I'm particularly struck by the way she uses time. The whole piece is a flashback, but inside the flashback she imagines her mother thinking ahead to the future, which is now the present:

It was not too long ago when my mother used to call me her sugarplum. Now that I'm older my mother says: "It seems like yesterday you were born, but here it is today and you're big."

She used to hold me in her arms, and sing me a song she knew. And when I was asleep she would just imagine how I would look when I grew up. When I was awake she would bathe me, and put a little pink ribbon in my hair, a pink dress, and white shoes with a pink puff flower. So when Daddy came home he would call me his princess. And then we'd go out.

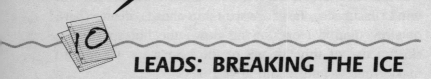

LEADS: BREAKING THE ICE

I recently spoke to Richard, a fifth grader, about his writing. "The hardest part for me is the beginning," Richard said. "I'm not good at it. Practically all my stories start with *one day* or something boring like that."

Talking with Richard got me thinking about beginnings: leads. By lead I mean the beginning of a piece of writing. Most leads are short, though a lead isn't limited to the first sentence, the first paragraph, or even the first page. (In *Hatchet* the lead lasts for several pages and involves that unforgettable ride in a bush plane when the pilot has a heart attack and Brian has to land the plane.) I used to think that the lead was just the mustard on the hot dog or the wrapping paper on the present—something you rip open to get at the important stuff inside.

I no longer think that's true. While the lead may not be the most important element of writing, it does give you an opportunity to set the tone early, to establish a rhythm and energy for what will follow.

You get invited to a new friend's house, a place you have never before visited. You ring the doorbell. Soon you find yourself standing inside the front door. What is it like? Right away you start noticing sweet smells from the kitchen, a baby crying, music playing, the floors dirty or shining clean. All of these clues tell you about what this family is like.

Writing is the same way. A lead gives the reader important clues about what to expect in the writing that will follow.

Let's take a look at some different kinds of leads, and how you can make them work for you.

THE "GRABBER LEAD"

William Steig's picture book *Shrek!* begins like this:

His mother was ugly and his father was ugly, but Shrek was uglier than the two of them put together. By the time he toddled, Shrek could spit flame a full ninety yards and vent smoke from either ear. With just a look he cowed the reptiles in the swamp. Any snake dumb enough to bite him instantly got convulsions and died.

How does Steig manage to hook me so quickly? This lead introduces a character I *know* I don't want to mess with. The first sentence seizes my attention and forces me to sit up straight. The next one, about Shrek spitting flame ninety yards, tells me that this will definitely not be a work of realistic fiction. Anything could happen in this book. The language in this lead is vivid, and the whole thing has an offbeat sense of humor that makes me chuckle even as I gasp.

You might decide to craft a lead that throws the reader headlong into the pool of your writing—no time to get used to the water temperature, whoops! there you go. You can do this by beginning with a dramatic scene, an excellent way to grab your reader's attention. Such scenes often use dialogue, which gives us the sneaky pleasure of eavesdropping on a conversation. *On My Honor*, by Marion Dane Bauer, begins like this:

"Climb the Starved Rock Bluffs? You've got to be kidding!" Joel's spine tingled at the mere thought of trying to scale the sheer river bluffs in the state park. He looked Tony square in the eye. "Somebody got killed last year trying to do that! Don't you remember?"

Speech like this is pretty hard to resist. The spoken words in the first paragraph hold enough fear, conflict, and promised drama to make me keep reading.

But you don't necessarily have to begin with fireworks. Another way of grabbing the reader is to write a lead that asks an intriguing question: "Did you know that for every white blood cell you have five hundred red blood cells?" Or: "Do you realize that we drink the same water the dinosaurs drank? There is only a certain amount of water on our planet, and that's why it is so important to keep that water clean."

Some writing grabs us because of a surprise at the very beginning. Note the tension between the first and second lines in this poem by Kamele Bento, a Hawaiian sixth grader:

I sang
When he died
He sang
I fell
Into a deep sleep
His skin was old
And crinkly
Like an old worn rug
No one could replace
His warm close hugs
He would always

81

Squeeze me so tight
Death fell on him quickly
But his spirit continues
I was his favorite Grand child
"You are as sweet as chocolate"
He would always say
I haven't stopped singing
He hasn't died in my heart
Good-bye doesn't mean forever
It's just a moment of time

INTRODUCING THE NARRATOR

Grabber leads are terrific, but sometimes you don't want to begin with neon lights. There will be times when you'll want something a little calmer, a little less ambitious. Some leads do nothing more than establish who is telling the story. Sarah Whitley, a sixth grader, begins one story with this lead:

Driving along it felt like every other trip we take, long and boring. I was just listening to a tape on my headphones when my mom muttered something which I could hardly hear to my brother and sister. I didn't think it was important until my brother said: "Cool."

The language in this lead is ordinary, almost dull. The first two sentences lull me into complacency and set up the little surprise at the end of the paragraph. The brother's comment—"Cool"—provides just enough of a hook to make me want to find out what will happen next.

Many professional writers begin their books in this low-key way. Will Hobbs begins his novel *Changes in Latitudes* with Travis, a fourteen-year-old, starting to tell the story: "We were leaving for a week in Mexico, all of us except my father, that is." This first sentence holds a small surprise about the missing father. Right away I want to know why the father isn't going on vacation with everyone else.

Cliff Abernathy is the narrator in my novel *Fig Pudding*. I wanted readers to get comfortable with Cliff as soon as possible, so I wrote a lead that had him introduce himself, speaking directly to the reader:

My full name is Clifford Allyn Abernathy III, after my father and grandfather, but I leave off the III, the Allyn, and the ord. Call me Cliff. I'm in Mr. Beck's class at the Bradford Bridges Elementary School in Ballingsford. I've noticed lately that lots of my favorite things seem to start with "B": baseball (Baltimore is my favorite team), basketball, bacon, bluefishing, blue slush cones. Brad.

THE MOODY LEAD

The beginning mood in a piece of writing could be compared with the background music you hear at the start of a movie. That music—whether ominous, offbeat, or cheerful—gives you a pretty accurate idea of what kind of movie you'll be watching.

Many books begin with a description of a place that sets the mood for what is to follow. A lead like this can be a sly way of introducing one of the themes in a book. Natalie Babbitt's book *Tuck Everlasting* starts off with a marvelous description of the first week of August, which "hangs at the very top of summer, the top of the live-long year, like the seat of a ferris wheel when it pauses in its turning." It's not accidental that this feeling of being stuck in time is one of the book's major themes.

My first picture book, *Twilight Comes Twice,* explores two magical times during the day, dawn and dusk. The book is soft and sensual, and I knew for certain that I didn't want a big, showy lead. I wanted a quiet lead that would help readers anticipate the kind of book that would follow. Here's what I came up with:

Twice each day
a crack opens
between night and day.

Twice twilight
slips through that crack.

It stays only a short time
while night and day
standing whispering secrets
before they go their
separate ways.

Your options for writing your lead are almost limit-less. If you study the works of our best writers you'll find that they use all kinds of ways to hook the reader.

• *Sound effects*: "BOOM! BOOM! Ka-BOOM! My big brother thundered down the stairs."

• *Narrative lead*: Nothing hooks the reader like a short, punchy story.

• *Misleading lead*: "The camping trip started on a per-fect October day, the skies emerald blue with just the hint of a chill in the air." (Don't you just know trouble will follow?)

• *Beginning at the end*: "We sat in the intensive care waiting room while I kept thinking of my father, fighting for his life inside. The day had started peacefully."

• *Disturbing fact or statistic*: "By the time you finish reading this article, a thousand acres of rain forest . . ."

• *Sentence fragments*: Grammatically incorrect, true. But sentence fragments can be a startlingly effective way to intrigue the reader. Alex Woods, a fourth grader in Ohio, wrote a short essay that begins like this:

When I Grow Up

In the lab. Peaceful silence. And then, machines clanking. Me. Inventing. Ever since age three I knew I wanted to be a scientist . . .

A few final things to consider as you craft your lead: This chapter makes a big fuss over the lead, but don't get hung up on it while you're writing your first draft. You don't even have to write the lead first. With *Fig Pudding* I had to finish the whole novel before I could go back and decide what kind of lead I wanted. The last thing I did was take out some paper and try out five or six leads until I found the right one. If the lead isn't coming the way you want, skip ahead into the meat of the writing. You can always come back to it. It will be the first thing your reader reads, but it doesn't have to be the first thing you write.

Remember that all your leads won't be showstoppers,

and they shouldn't be. You're not trying to win the Olympic gold medal of lead-writing. The goal is simply to come up with the right lead to the writing on which you're working.

Don't despair if all your leads tend to sound alike at some time. All writers get stuck in ruts. Experiment! Think of it this way: As a writer, you've got one of those enormous boxes of crayons with a hundred and twenty-eight colors, hues that range from burnt sienna to jelly-bean pink. With so many to choose from, why color with the same old green every time?

THE END:
GETTING THE LAST WORD

I once took my wife to a fancy restaurant that serves the most succulent blackened swordfish in the world. The restaurant was expensive, but I didn't care: it was our wedding anniversary and I was willing to splurge. We sailed through the first four dinner courses (fresh oysters, lobster bisque, Caesar salad, swordfish) and each ordered chocolate mousse pie for dessert. As I took my first bite of the chocolate mousse pie I was shocked to feel a stab of pain on the inside of my lip.

"You're bleeding!" my wife said. I felt something sharp inside my mouth, and we were both astonished when I pulled out a piece of glass. I called the maître d' over to our table and showed it to him.

"What if I had swallowed that?" I squawked. The maître d' was extremely apologetic and told us that the restaurant would pay our bill. Even so, we never went back to that place again.

That glass-in-the-mousse incident ruined our dinner. It didn't matter that the rest of the food was delicious. What mattered most (I'll never forget it) was what happened at the end of the meal.

Endings matter in writing, too. How many times have you been engrossed in a book only to find that the story falls apart at the very end? This can happen in a dozen different ways: the story gets sappy, goes on too long, or teases you by leaving you hanging so you have to go out and buy the next book in the series.

Some years ago I was working on a collection of water poems. We had just celebrated the birth of my son Robert, so my writing often got interrupted by crying, feedings, etc. One day I got the idea of combining the two subjects—water and babies—in one poem:

Babies

Faucets drip
Pools cool
Springs bubble
Babies drool

Seas sparkle ·
Waves crash
Streams gurgle
Babies splash

Rivers rise
Flood and worse
Lakes glisten
Babies nurse

Ice melts
Cold creeks
Hail pelts
Babies leak

People laugh when I read this out loud at a poetry reading. This is my idea of a *humorous ending*, something I often try to use in both my writing and my speeches. Most people hunker down into a state of concentration when they read; this kind of ending catches readers off-guard by tickling their funny bone instead of their intellect.

I had one very funny incident I knew I was going to use in my first novel, *Fig Pudding*, though I didn't know where to use it. (In the story, the family makes fig pudding and brings a bowl of it to a holiday dinner. The youngest child steps in the bowl of fig pudding, but the father convinces the rest of the family they can bring it in and serve it anyway.) This book has two chapters in the middle that are so sad some teachers actually cry while reading them to their students. Instead of ending the book on a sad note, I decided to have a humorous ending. But how should I write it? I didn't want one of those cheap, tacked-on happy endings you see so often on TV. I decided to use the incident with the bowl of fig pudding. Even though this ending gives the book a bit of a roller-coaster shape—up, down, up— it allowed me to leave the reader with laughter.

Here's a tip for trying a humorous ending. Read over your rough draft and put a star next to the funniest part. See if you can save that part to use at the very end.

The late Harry Chapin wrote a song that begins: "All my life's a circle, sunrise and sundown." I agree, and it's true in writing as well. Many familiar poems and stories have *circular endings*. The picture book *If You Give a Mouse a Cookie*, for example, uses the last line of the book to bring us right back to the beginning.

It's easy to see why so many writers use the circular ending in their writing. When it's done well, a circular ending leaves the reader with a satisfied feeling. This kind of ending gives the piece balance. By tying together the beginning and the end, a circular ending makes the writing feel whole.

Some authors use a circular ending to return to the

actual beginning of the writing. But you can also take a detail or incident from the beginning of the story and return to it at the end. That's what happens in Steven Kellogg's picture book *Best Friends*. On the first page we read about two girls who are close friends. The girls dream of owning a stallion and naming it Golden Silverwind. Near the end the girls are excited about a neighbor's dog who is just about to have puppies. Each girl plans to adopt one, but it turns out that the dog has only one puppy.

The story has a perfect resolution: in the end they decide to share the dog. And they decide to name him Golden Silverwind.

Circular endings can be used in all kinds of writing: poems, reports, essays, stories. But this kind of ending must be set up ahead of time or it will not work. You have to feed your reader an early detail or incident early in your writing so you can come back to it in the end.

A few years ago some close friends told me this story about their two-year-old son. He and his big brother were racing through the house and slammed hard into a wall in their kitchen.

"He split his head open!" the older boy cried—not exactly true, though there was a deep gash on his forehead. The father picked up the screaming child and drove him to the emergency room at the hospital. Two hours, three stitches, and one ice-cream cone later they were all back home again. The house was calm several hours later when the boys' mother came home from work.

"My God, what happened?" she cried when she saw the bandage on his head.

"Tell Mommy what happened," the father said to the two-year-old. At this the boy ran full speed—*Bang!*—into the same wall he'd smashed into five hours earlier. His head wound reopened, and they had to rush back to the hospital.

This story has a *surprise ending,* which is my favorite flavor of finale. Is there anything better than that "Whoa! What's going on?" feeling of being totally surprised, startled, shocked at the end of a story? Give me one final nasty twist and I'm in heaven.

But surprise endings aren't quite as easy as they look. You have to carefully plan the surprise ending in order for it to work. I interviewed Jane Yolen (author of *Owl Moon*) about surprise endings, and she put it this way: "The seed for a surprise ending has to be planted early in the story."

Read books with surprise endings so you can study how they work. Check out *White Dynamite and Curly Kidd* by Bill Martin and John Archambault. Or take a look at *Charlie Anderson*, a picture book by Barbara Abercrombie. Both books have surprises (I don't want to spoil them) that are carefully set up by the authors with information provided earlier in the text.

Have you ever read a poem or book that brings you close to tears, or makes you cry? Recently I read *A Taste of Blackberries* by Doris Buchanan Smith. This story is about the friendship between two boys. While picking blackberries, the boy named Jamie gets stung by a bee, has an allergic reaction, and dies. In the rest of the book we watch the boy trying to deal with Jamie's tragic death. At the very end, he goes back to the blackberry patch, picks some blackberries, and brings them to Jamie's mother as a gift.

An *emotional ending* like this is a powerful writing tool. Such endings don't have to be complicated: you can use simple language but still pack an emotional wallop. Who can forget the last paragraph in *Charlotte's Web*, in which Wilbur is thinking back on Charlotte:

It's a rare thing to find someone who is both a good friend and a good writer. Charlotte was both.

I encourage you to experiment, trying different kinds of endings until you find one that fits with the rest of the text. There's no reason why you can't take different kind of endings and combine them. Micah Botello, a Hawaiian sixth grader, writes an ending that is both circular and emotional in this stirring tribute to her uncle:

Uncle Moku, I Love You

My Uncle Moku used to pull weeds on his hands and knees in the hot burning sun. He liked wearing his long white pants and old cowboy hat to keep the sun out of his eyes. He was an old chubby man with skeleton looking teeth, short white beard, and puka tank tops. One morning he had a heart attack. I was so, so sad. How I wish he was here so I could listen to his loud laugh. I would like to sit at the dinner table and taste his hot chilipepper sauce. Now our garden has nothing but weeds. I'm trying to follow his lead, start what he could not finish, and start pulling. I think he liked pulling weeds, and I think I do, too.

Micah chooses a small detail—pulling weeds—to end her tribute. A small detail like that can be an excellent way to create an emotional ending.

Here are a few ending thoughts about endings:

• *Trust your reader.* An ending gets weakened when the author states something obvious to the reader. For example, one young writer wrote a terrific story about the death of a beloved dog. Here is his last paragraph:

We sat around the living room. Every person in the family had a small pile of used up tissues in front of them. But the pile in front of my mother was the biggest one of all. She loved the dog more than anyone else.

As a writer, you must trust the reader. Give just enough information so the reader can grasp what you're trying to say. This author has already chosen a compelling detail to dramatize the fact that the mother loved the dog the most. The story would be stronger without that last sentence.

• *Don't make your ending do too much.* Remember, the goal isn't to devise the Greatest Ending Ever Written. You're just trying to come up with the right ending for what you're writing.

So far we have explored the kind of striking endings that will leave a deep impression on the reader. But there may be times when you don't want to make a big deal about the ending. My picture book *Twilight Comes Twice* tries to capture the magical feeling of dawn and dusk. Here's the very last page:

As you set your table for breakfast
dawn is setting its own table

with light that will usher in
a brand new day.

This page isn't as lyrical as the rest of the text, but
that's all right. I wanted to end the book in a way that
would keep the quiet mood intact. I was trying to make
a graceful exit. More than anything else I didn't want
to do any damage on the way out.

Endings matter. In fact, I consider the ending to be
every bit as important as the lead, maybe more so because its words will be the last to echo in the ear of
the reader. I usually try to give the reader something at
the end: a memorable quote, statement, or idea that will
linger in the mind. Sam Hundt, an Ohio sixth grader,
does exactly that in this short passage:

People are stars. From far away they all seem
to be the same. But they are all different sizes and
shapes. Each one shines on a small part of a huge
galaxy, and each one shines for its own purpose.
But still, from where we lie they are just speckles
in the sky. We could all move a little closer and
find why each one twinkles so bright.

THE SMALL IMPORTANT THINGS

Years ago two of my younger brothers, ages two and three, went out in the front yard. They began looking for things, and for some fool reason, they took it into their heads to eat whatever they found. They ate some dandelions. They munched grass, chewed sticks, swallowed dirt. They pried some used gum off the sidewalk and put it in their mouths. They found a discarded cigarette, broke it in half, and snacked on that.

An hour later they staggered into the house, crying and holding their bellies. My mother took them to the hospital, where they got their stomachs pumped. They survived, but I still think back on the day my little brothers decided to eat the world.

This story is pretty nauseating, but there's a lesson in it for writers. If I had just written "They went outside and started eating the stuff they found on the ground" and left it at that, the story wouldn't have had much punch. The gruesome details of exactly what they ate make this story both revolting and unforgettable.

There is a crazy notion floating around that writers stay above it all, more concerned with lofty ideas and five-syllable words than with the messy particulars of life. I couldn't disagree more. Details are the lifeblood of writing. Learning to use details is a dramatic way to breathe new life into your writing. Here are some important ways to do just that.

Write low on the food chain. Writers take great delight in all the particulars of the world. Recently I had to take my car to a mechanic to get the radiator checked. The man groaned as soon as he opened the hood.

"What's wrong?" I asked.

"You're from up north, ain't you?" he asked.

"Yes," I admitted. "New Hampshire. How'd you know?"

"See all this corrosion here?" he asked, pointing at the engine. "It's from all the salt they put on the road on account of the snow. Salt really does a number on a car, 'specially the body."

In school I learned about the food chain of life: small bacteria get eaten by larger bacteria, who get eaten by krill, who get devoured by tiny fish, who get preyed upon by larger fish, who get eaten by people . . . In writing there is also a food chain of ideas, which looks something like this:

Main idea

Supporting Ideas
Underlying details

Note that in the writing food chain the most general ideas are on top and the most specific details are at the bottom. Most people, adults as well as kids, tend to write too high on the food chain. They write about big ideas—jealousy, love, nuclear war—instead of seeking out small details to suggest the larger issue. In the past few years I have seen real improvement in my writing simply because I have tried to stay low on the food chain when I write.

If you want to learn to write small you need to get the knack of selecting odd details that will stick in the reader's mind. Look at the details in this story written by Jane Wright, a seventh grader in Maine:

Beep, beep, beep. As I slam off the alarm I look up at the clock, 6:15 A.M. I think to myself: well, here comes another long day of school. As I slowly push myself out of bed I stumble around my room in complete darkness. I wonder what it would look like if I could see myself do that one day. Can you imagine how insane that would look?

After I have succeeded in doing that I find the bathroom. I pull back my hair and turn on the water. I take big bowls of water in my hands and splash my face. I swear the water has to be colder than the ice on the trees outside. I immediately turn off the water and reach for the closest towel near me. The towel is cream-colored and has little red, blue, and green flowers on it. They are the towels Mom and Dad got when they were married. So obviously they are out of style.

Normally I wouldn't be much interested in hearing about someone's morning routine, but the author has selected odd details that make this piece pleasurable to read.

Use details to make complex ideas understandable. In *Yolanda's Genius,* by Carol Fenner, Yolanda's mother is tired of the crime and other perils of living in urban Chicago. Ideas like crime, safety, and danger all live pretty high on the food chain of ideas, but Carol

Fenner finds a way to dramatize them through a few well-chosen details:

> She [Yolanda's mother] was always talking about growing flowers and owning a barbecue grill they wouldn't have to chain to the house.

Pick details that create vivid pictures for the reader. Details create the images in your writing, but be careful you don't go overboard and bury your reader in mountains of trivia. Instead, try to dig up the odd details that will stick in the reader's mind. Look at this description of a new baby:

> For the first year she didn't have any hair at all, and we taped a pink bow to the top of her head.

The Watsons go to Birmingham—1963, by Christopher Curtis, is a novel full of odd, wonderful details:

> The only problem with having two pairs of gloves was that if you lost one you had to wear the next pair kindergarten-style. That meant Momma would run a string through the sleeves of your coat and tie two safety pins on the ends of the string, then she'd pin your gloves to the string and it was im-

possible to lose the gloves because every time you took them off they'd just hang from your coat.

I remember the embarrassment of having to wear gloves ''kindergarten-style'' because I'd lost a previous pair. This detail, familiar yet somehow fresh, gives readers a crystal-clear window into the Watsons' family life.

Select details that make your writing sound authentic. Check out this excerpt from a story about car racing, written by Micah Botelho, a sixth grader in Honolulu:

I'm running against Hawaiian Thunder, one of the fastest cars on the track. My pitman gives me the signal; he drops his hand. I slam my foot hard on the gas pedal. All my gizmos and gadgets are going. My slicks (tires) spin, burning like rubber. All of a sudden it's over. I finish the stage. I pull up to the start line, my foot hard on the brake, and wait for the light, feeling eager because once the light hits green I'M BAD!

All of a sudden, BOOM!, it's green. I pound the gas. I glance at Thunder's car just one fender in front of me. I accelerate, fuel burning, speedometer crazy, rpms blasting, everything flying.

I don't know the first thing about car racing, but the details in this story convince me that this narrator really knows the world of car racing.

Finding details is pretty easy if you're writing about something you already know lots about. But you may find yourself writing about a new subject, lacking concrete details. If that happens, you may need a crash course in your topic. All kinds of writers, including poets, research their subjects. As you research, try to dig up plenty of specific details to make the writing sound believable.

Important details often show up again later in the writing. We already looked at the circular ending, but you can also choose details that show up later in the writing. Recurring details can act as the glue to hold together a piece of writing. For instance, my book *I Am Wings: Poems About Love* has two sections—"Falling In" and "Falling Out." Here's one of the poems from the first section:

Space

How you hated
the little gap
small extra   space
between your front teeth.

But I wanted to say:
Leave that space.
Let it be.

Leave space
in your life
for me.

At the end of the book, in the "Falling Out" section, there is a poem called "Lies, Lies," which is written as a nasty note from one kid to another. At the end of the note, the speaker returns to that gap in the teeth that had once seemed so cute and tender:

PS Forget what I said
about the space
in your teeth.
You really should
get that fixed.

Don't be afraid to invent details. Have you ever opened one of those sticks of gray clay you get at an art store? At first the clay is hard to work with. You have to hold it in your hand, warm and soften it up. After you have worked the clay in this fashion you can start shaping it: hammering it flat, breaking off pieces, rolling it into a ball.

The same thing is true about writing. Think of your writing topic as your clay. As a writer, you must take this clay into your hands, warm it up, and begin to shape it. It took me a long time to learn this myself. Writers don't just write down everything that happens to them. Writers shape their material.

How do you shape it? Let's say you are basing your writing on something that happened. In the writing you can alter what really happened to make the poem or story work better. This may include adding or changing the details from the original event. That's exactly what I did in *Fig Pudding*. At the beginning of that novel the Abernathy family gathers to admire the buds on the Christmas cactus. Later there is a tragic death in the story, and I wanted some way of dramatizing this death. I gave myself permission to invent by playing the "what if" game with the details of the story. The death had taken place just a few months before Christmas. What if, I wondered, the Christmas cactus didn't bloom that year? It didn't happen this way in real life, but I wrote it that way in the book and I think it makes the story much stronger.

What if you are writing a poem or story based on a true event, but you can't remember an important detail? Give yourself permission to invent. Make it up. Maybe you can't remember what your grandfather wore the last time you saw him, but if you write with convincing details—"He was wearing his favorite green corduroy vest, and there was a faint smell of pipe tobacco about him"—your readers will believe you.

Life is messy, and as a writer you can't afford to stay above the mess. There's no way around it: writers get dirty. Roll up your sleeves and plunge your hands into the details, because nine times out of ten that's where you'll find the lifeblood of the writing. Listen to the details my friend Thomas uses to describe making peach ice cream at his grandmother's house:

"You got to keep turning the hand crank, and it's hard, lemme tell you, your arm's fixin' to fall off you're so tired, but you gotta keep going 'cause that peach ice cream's gotta get made. And when it's ready, oh man! You take three quick bites and it's so cold your head starts poundin' right here [touches his forehead], but you've never tasted nothin' that good, so you just keep eatin', and meanwhile the yellow jackets are going so wild smelling all the sweet ice they start dive-bombing the ice-cream machine. I'm tellin' you! They're willin' to commit suicide just for one tiny taste of that ice cream so they can die happy, and I can't hardly blame 'em."

13

THE GOLDEN LINE

It can happen anywhere: in a novel, short story, article, or poem. You are cruising along when all of a sudden—wham!—you come across an amazing sentence that nearly knocks you over. It can even happen in a picture book like *The Relatives Came,* by Cynthia Rylant. In one part of that book all the relatives are sleeping together, and Rylant writes: "It was different going to sleep with all that new breathing in the house."

A sweet sentence like that makes you sit up straight, go back, and read it all over again.

Beautiful sentences. I have heard people describe them as golden lines. A golden line doesn't have to be very long. In fact, it doesn't even have to be a sentence. Brooke Madewell, a sixth grade writer, has this description in a story: "slashes of light pour into my room."

Brooke's classmate Ashlie McAvene has written a poem, "Pain," about a beloved old relative. It begins like this:

I wish I could
feel your pain
your silence
your face.
I wish I could feel your worn down light
your worn down battery.

Golden lines like these do at least two things: they breathe instant life into any piece of writing, and they work as a wake-up call to your reader. True, some people seem to have a knack for writing sentences that sparkle, but everyone can learn how to write memorable sentences.

Here are a few tips for creating golden lines in your writing:

Use strong verbs. Oh, brother, you're probably thinking, not verbs again! Anything but verbs! Okay, so your teachers have been urging you to use strong verbs since you were in first grade, right? Well, in this case they happen to be right. I'm not going to make a big fuss about adverbs and adjectives (I think they're over-rated, if you want to know the truth), but the right verb can make an enormous difference in a piece of writing.

Look at the image created in this poem by Melissa Fitzwater, a sixth grader:

The Sun Dissolves

The sun dissolves over
the horizon under the
big blue ocean and makes
millions of little sparkles
in the water.
Up in the high mountain
tops you can't tell where
heaven begins and the
sun dissolves.

In *A Writer's Notebook,* I included an excerpt from Thomas Powning, a fifth grader who wrote about the immensity of space. He had one sentence that went like this: "*Clamp* your hands on your ears, *make* me stop, the wonders will (   ) us all!"

Take a guess: what verb do you think Thomas used in this sentence? *Amaze? Affect? Astonish? Thrill?* All those words would do just fine, but Thomas chose a truly remarkable verb in this context: *infest.* "*Clamp* your hands on your ears, *make* me stop, the wonders will *infest* us all!'' That surprising verb transforms a very good sentence into a great one.

Try a surprising comparison. A simile is a poetic device in which two things are compared using *like* or *as:* ''My uncle fell asleep on the couch, snoring like a chain saw cutting down some faraway forest.'' Metaphors are similar except that the comparison is implied: ''The small children buzzed around the candy in a frenzied swarm.''

Metaphors and similes are among the most powerful tools you have as a writer. You can jump-start some humdrum writing by boldly comparing two things that don't seem to go together. David Uy, an Ohio sixth grader, does this in the following passage he wrote:

I am like a match, and my bed is like a match box. Every morning I get taken out of that box and lit. That light is the light of day: I am the light of the day. But when night comes I am nothing. I fill the air with that smoldering smoke of night, which leaves the mystery of the dreams that have been lost. But always in the morning I get struck again. And out comes the light, the light I have given away.

James Albrecht, who is also a sixth grader, paints a

vivid mind picture with this surprising metaphor: "She is digging into her crayon box like she's taking candy out of a bowl."

Athena Biggs, another sixth grader, uses a lovely metaphor in this poem which consists of a single sentence:

Stars

Are stars
really angels
lost souls
who have nowhere
to go,
just watching
over the world
like fairy godmothers?

Beware overwriting. I'm wild about just about any kind of chocolates, but my favorite is dark chocolate truffles. *Mmmm,* my mouth waters just thinking about them. I try to stop eating them, I really do, but I can't. The first one goes down so easy the second one is in my hand before I have even thought about it. And that one tastes even better than the first. By the fourth truffle, my stomach has started feeling funny. That's a warning sign. I've learned that if I don't stop now I'll get a stomach ache. The same thing can happen with super-rich writing:

> When we got to the hospital my mom was jumpier than a Mexican jumping bean. But when we saw that Grandma was awake, Mom's face lit up like a lightbulb. And when Grandma hugged me, my heart lit up like a volcano ready to erupt.

This writing may be heartfelt, but it sure feels over-written to me. I barely have a chance to swallow one metaphor before—look out!—here comes another one. It reminds me of eating four chocolate truffles in a row: too much, too rich, too fast.

Overwriting is a problem many writers face at various times in their writing. I should know: I went through this stage myself. If one descriptive word helps a sentence, why not use three? Why limit yourself to one or two golden lines—how about a string of golden lines? It's logical, but wrong. This is a good way to turn off your readers.

I try not to censor my bold metaphors and flowery writing when I do a first draft. But I always go back over my writing at the end and cut out the lines or passages where the writing is too rich.

Sometimes I find that I wrote one wonderful sentence in a first draft but the rest of it is, well, pretty awful.

In this case the golden line sticks out. It is my challenge as a writer to integrate a fine line like this one into the rest of the work. I work hard to make the rest of the writing worthy of the golden line.

How many golden lines should you have? How many strong verbs do you need? How much descriptive language is enough? Or too much? There are no absolute answers to these questions. In the long run, you need to develop your own eye and ear for what makes good writing. This will give you a lens for going back and rereading what you have written.

Enjoy with me this passage by Emma Yuen, a fifth grader in Hilo, Hawaii. I admire Emma's sensual descriptions and the verbs she uses to make them come alive.

Flying

Wings a beautiful bounty of white feathers at the blades of my back. Lifting airborne rising up choking with happiness. Tears running down my face, love, beating wind. Going higher the cool air caresses me and my silk satin dress warms my torso. I am pure. I feel purified and filled with ecstatic love. I am giddy and I calm myself down. I explore my wings and see how fast I can go racing. I leap, I fly, I love. I can't believe the beauty of the wonderful Earth. I go to a waterfall and sweep down springing the droplets on my face. I am like an angel, I think. I will never stop. I will remain airborne and pure. I am flying. I am so happy. Sigh! I am daydreaming.

PUTTING IT ALL TOGETHER

So far we've been trying to break writing down into its parts so we can examine them separately. It's important to do that, but it's also important to remember that these individual parts don't matter by themselves. A lead, ending, or conflict can't survive on its own. The elements of writing work only as part of a whole.

Let's look at a longer piece of writing where we can see all the writing elements (lead, voice, character, conflict, ending) working together. At first I thought of choosing a published piece of writing by a professional author, but in the end I thought it might be more interesting to look at a narrative written by a student. The writing in this piece isn't perfect—you may not even like the story—but I believe it's a work we can all learn from. Let's read it twice, once to enjoy it, and a second time to see what it can teach about good writing. This story was written by Elissa Bosley, a seventh grader in Maine.

Angie

1   I guess you could say my sister Angie's different. I guess you could say she just doesn't fit in. Or, at least that's what it looked like through my eyes. Sadly I didn't see the real Angie until I was fifteen.

2   "Angie! Mom, could you please keep her out of my room!" The chubby little hand reached for my twenty-dollar hairbrush and I lashed at it in a frustrated rage.

3   "No, Angie!"

4   "I'm not supposed to play with Mary's things," she said with a sigh as she placed the brush down as if it were the most delicate egg.

5   "Yes, Angie, Mary doesn't like to share," my mother said, speaking in that soothing calming tone parents always use. I hadn't noticed her from the doorway where she had been witnessing the whole scene. She walked silently into the room and took my sister's hand. As she walked by she gave me that glare that said much

more than words could. Angie, who had once been excited and happy, was hunched over and sad.

6   "I know, let's go to the pond to feed the ducks!" a fake, excited voice said. My mother started to walk Angie out of the room and I listened as their murmurings continued down the carpeted hallway. Without even looking I knew that Angie was happy once again and was mumbling about taking her doll Bethany with her, and how much bread she should throw to the ducks.

7   I felt a so-familiar twinge of guilt as I turned back towards my expensive vanity. Maybe I should have been more understanding and have offered to take Angie to the pond myself. After all, my mother was with her all day, and many times she had to deal with my selfishness when I got home from school. Every time I had those feelings of guilt another feeling followed them— a feeling of longing. Many times I wished for a normal older sister. You know, the ones who braid your hair for you, teach you how to put on makeup, and give you advice on boys and things—kind of like the ones on those family TV shows that are always on in the afternoon. But I didn't have an older sister like that. I had one with Down's syndrome.

8   Later that afternoon I walked into our parlor and went to the heavy books on the dusty shelves—the photo albums. I don't think I've ever even looked at them once. They were just another thing that reminded me of my family. I slowly flipped through the sticky plastic pages staring at the smiling faces. In all of the pictures Angie had a huge grin on her face while I have one of those "I'm-not-having-fun-but-I'll-pretend-I-am" smiles. Even in our earliest years I could notice Angie's small head, upward slanting eyes, and small flat nose. All of these were caused by her disability. I hated it. I hated the pictures. More than anything I wanted to scream. I wanted to rip up the pictures and have them be gone forever. Then I heard the opening of a door followed by the happy voices. I suppressed my anger and walked to my room. I pushed the photo album under my bed, still open to the last page I was looking at.

9   On a cold November day Angie got sick. It didn't surprise me that much. She was always getting sick from time to time. My mother told me that this time she wasn't just sort of sick, she was really sick, hospital sick. My mother had to spend most of her time at the hospital and that meant less time for me. I just wanted her to get

back soon so my life could get back to as normal as possible.

10   I heard the doctors say once that she needed a heart transplant. After I heard that, the sinking feelings of guilt and longing came back. I guess I tried to tell myself that I wasn't visiting her because I didn't have the time, but the truth was I was afraid, afraid of those feelings. After the second week Angie was in the hospital, my mother made me go visit her.

11   "So how's the food?" I said to break the silence.

12   "Good," replied the same cheery voice I had always known. "Let's play dolls," Angie suggested. I nodded. Angie pointed to a pink My Little Pony bag that lay beside her bed. I reached inside and pulled out the various Barbie dolls.

13   "I'll be the blond."

14   "I'll be the brunette." The same conversation continued. I felt very nervous. The walls were too white and it almost seemed like they were closing in on me. And even though the window-sills were covered with flowers and new toys, it just didn't look right. Then suddenly, out of no-where, she asked it. She asked the most horrible question she could have asked.

15 "Why don't you like me, Mary?"

16 I didn't know what to do. My throat went dry and there was a huge lump in it. Even if I had wanted to answer it wouldn't have been possible. It would have been so simple to say that I did like her and just didn't have time to spend with her. But something was stopping me. Her deep blue eyes were staring right at me begging for an answer. I opened my mouth. Silence.

17 "I guess I'm afraid," I finally choked out.

18 "Why?" Somehow I knew that was coming. But then something saved me, or didn't save me. My mother walked into the room ready to take me home.

19 "Good-bye, Angie," I said as I closed the heavy door behind me. All I could hear as I walked down the hall were the clicking sounds of the heels of my shoes on the hard linoleum. Everything else seemed not to be there.

20 When I got home that evening I ran right to my room. I needed time to think. I sat on my floor and started rocking back and forth. I stared at the rug. Everything looked blurry. I started wondering if I got to know her better, or talked to her like any other person, my feelings would change. Maybe Angie was all right and I just

121

never realized it. Maybe there was more to her than what I saw on the outside.

21   As I continued rocking back and forth I noticed something I had left in my room for at least four months. The photo album under my bed. I pulled it out and studied the picture that I had had been looking at that day long ago. I saw my fake smile and the way I wasn't really in the picture. But I also saw Angie's twinkling eyes, bright smile, and her really truly happy face. I started to carefully pull away the sticky plastic covering. I took the picture out. Instead of ripping it up as I had wanted to four months earlier, I stood up and walked over to my vanity. I wedged the corner of the picture into the side of my mirror. There it was. My family—out for everyone to see.

Let's reread ''Angie'' so we can take a closer look at how Elissa wrote it. I'm going to say how each part of the story affects me. You may not agree—two readers often see different things in the same piece of writing—but my reactions will at least provide a starting point. I'll go paragraph by paragraph, so you'll have to flip back and forth.

1: This lead grabs my attention. We learn in the first sentence that Angie's different—I'm wondering how. I'm eager to read ahead so I can find out. She repeats ''I guess'' to begin the first two sentences. That builds a rhythm. At first I thought this would be a profile of her sister, but the third and fourth sentences give me a clue that the ''I,'' the narrator, will also be a big part of the story.

2: The author quickly brings us into a scene where we can observe the conflict between these two sisters. *Chubby little hand* is a detail I can picture, and the word *lashed* is full of anger. This author carefully selects her details, mentioning that the hairbrush cost twenty dollars, for instance.

4: Note how carefully Angie puts down the brush.

5: This paragraph introduces the mother. Her comment to Angie—Mary doesn't like to share— is directed at the sister telling the story.

6: The last sentence in this paragraph tells us that the narrator has been through other scenes exactly like this one.

7: A very important paragraph. Up until now I figured that the conflict in this story was between the two sisters. But now the narrator is letting us know what's going on inside her. She shares her feelings—guilt, regret, longing—in a way that feels totally honest.

This paragraph ends with the bombshell: ''I

didn't have an older sister like that. I had one with Down's syndrome.'' These are what I call heavy sentences, but the author doesn't belabor them. She states the facts and moves on.

There are lots of great details in this paragraph: all the simple things she wishes her sister could do for her. The ''expensive vanity'' is the second mention where the focus is on money. I wonder if the narrator is making a comment on her own value system where materialism gets valued over her relationship with her sister.

8: In this paragraph she looks at the photo albums. I'm struck again by her total honesty as she describes her fake smiles. In the middle of the paragraph she uses a series of short sentences: ''I hated it. I hated the pictures. More than anything I wanted to scream.'' An occasional short sentence can really pack a punch in the middle of longer sentences.

More great details: the sticky plastic pages, and the fact that when she pushes the photo album under her bed it is still open to the last page.

9: Angie gets sick. I love the sentence: ''My mother told me that this time she wasn't just sort of sick, she was really sick, hospital sick.'' This sentence builds on itself and becomes more and more ominous through repetition of the word *sick*.

Again, the narrator is brutally honest about herself—she wants Angie to get better mostly so she can get more attention from her mother.

11: This is the second scene in this story. It begins in the most ordinary way imaginable, chatting about the hospital food.

12: Simple details about playing dolls. I get the feeling that these sisters rarely play together. I can feel how much Angie would like to play with her sister, and how much the narrator wishes Angie would just disappear.

14: Here the author doesn't bore us with every last thing the girls said as they played dolls. Instead she summarizes the dialogue (''The same conversation continued.'') and moves on to focus our attention on the eerie details of that hospital room. We get the narrator's strong feeling of claustrophobia. And then she hits us with the set-up sentence: ''She asked me the most horrible question she could have asked.''

15: The whole piece has been building up to this simple question: ''Why don't you like me?''

16: The narrator wrestles with how to answer this question. She considers copping out by lying, but she's too honest for that. I think this is why I like this narrator. True, she can be nasty and mean-spirited, but she's willing to look at herself and ask honest, soul-searching questions. Her honesty lets me overlook (or at least tolerate) her selfishness.

18: ''But then something saved me, or didn't save me.'' This sentence is great, wonderfully complex. I don't completely understand it, but it sure does make me think. I think the narrator is trying to say that even though she got spared from responding to Angie's question, she realized that she needed to answer it.

19: The narrator does a great job of describing the hospital as she leaves Angie's room: the ''heavy door . . . the clicking sound of the heels of my shoes on the hard linoleum.'' These details are carefully selected to reveal her state of mind.

20: The author uses repetition and her honest voice: ''Maybe Angie was all right and I just never realized it. Maybe there was more to her than what I saw on the outside.''

21: In a kind of circular ending, the narrator returns to the photo album that was mentioned way back in paragraph 8. The power of the writing comes from its honesty: ''I saw my fake smile and the way I wasn't really in the picture.'' She takes out the photo and leaves it up for everyone to see.

It's important to know when to end a piece of writing. Many of us would be tempted to continue writing this story, perhaps come back to Angie and let the reader know if she gets better or worse. But doing so would run the risk of writing the life out of the story. I think the author made a wise decision here. The real story is not what happens to Angie. The real story is about what happens inside the narrator. Something has been resolved for the narrator. The picture she puts on her vanity is worth a thousand words that don't need to be written.

One final note: I asked Elissa Bosley how she came to write this story. In particular, I asked if the story was real. Here is what she told me:

I was thirteen and in the seventh grade when I wrote "Angie." I got the idea for the characters, Angie and Mary, because of my participation in the track program at school. There was a girl with Down's syndrome on the track team. She had an older brother who was an average student and I talked with him often. I began to observe how the girl acted and how her brother acted around her. He told me it was hard to have a sister who was so different, and that she was in and out of the hospital a lot. Although he was annoyed with her sometimes, he would do anything for her and everyone knew it. So, I guess this story is based on something real, the love of your sibling. Most of the story I imagined in my mind. Is it real? In my imagination, it is as real as you are.

I had to do a lot of research for this story. I studied Down's syndrome in fourth grade, but I had forgotten most of it. I like my stories to have true facts in them, so I had to check out many books on disabilities.

LAST THOUGHTS

In this book I've shared strategies you can use to improve the quality of your writing. I have tried to use a combination of practical ideas and lots of examples to help demystify writing. But it's hard to take all the mystery out of writing because there's still an undeniable magic in the air whenever a person puts pen to paper. A few years ago I tried to capture this magic in the following poem:

A Writing Kind of Day

It is raining today,
a writing kind of day.

Each word hits the page
like a drop in a puddle
and starts off
a tiny circle
of trembling feeling
that expands from the source
and slowly fades away.

As you continue to grow as a writer, I wish you
passion balanced with playfulness, perseverance balanced by patience, honesty balanced with humor.

And plenty of magic.

Never forget that writing is powerful stuff. Let's give
the final word to a young writer, a sixth grader named
Alaysha Vaugn who lives in the Bronx, New York:

Taking a Stand

How can we hold this troubled world?
Help each and every troubled man?
How can we live?

Today I stand impatiently waiting.
All we need is an independent woman
Like ME.
I shall be more than a girl.
TAKE ME AS I AM.
I can stand the pressure.
STAND ME ALONE.

Selected Reading

Babbitt, Natalie. *Tuck Everlasting*. Farrar, Straus, & Giroux 1975.

Bauer, Marion Dane. *On My Honor*. Bantam Doubleday Dell, 1987.

Borden, Louise. *Goodbye, Charles Lindbergh*. Simon & Schuster, 1998.

Borden, Louise. *Little Ships*. Simon & Schuster, 1997.

Coman, Carolyn. *Tell Me Everything*. Farrar, Straus, & Giroux, 1993.

Coman, Carolyn. *What Jamie Saw*. Front Street, 1995.

Curtis, Christopher Paul. *The Watsons Go To Birmingham—1963*. Bantam Doubleday Dell, 1995.

Fenner, Carol. *Yolanda's Genius*. Simon & Schuster, 1998.

Fletcher, Ralph. *Fig Pudding*. Houghton Mifflin, 1995.

Fletcher, Ralph. *Flying Solo*. Houghton Mifflin, 1998.

Fletcher, Ralph. *I Am Wings: Poems About Love*. Simon & Schuster, 1994.

Fletcher, Ralph. *Spider Boy*. Houghton Mifflin, 1997.

Fletcher, Ralph. *Twilight Comes Twice*. Houghton Mifflin, 1997.

Fletcher, Ralph. *A Writer's Notebook*. Avon Books, 1996.

George, Jean Craighead. *My Side of the Mountain*. Dutton's Children's Books, 1991.

Hobbs, Will. *Changes In Latitudes*. Avon Books, 1992.

Kellogg, Steven. *Best Friends*. Dial Books for Young Readers, 1986.

London, Jack. *The Call Of The Wild*. Pocket Books, 1982.

Lyons, Mary E. *Letters From a Slave Girl*. Simon & Schuster, 1995.

Martin Jr., Bill and Archambault, John. *White Dynamite and Curly Kidd*. Henry Holt, 1989.

Myers, Walter Dean. *Slam!* Scholastic, 1996.

Nolan, Han. *Dancing on the Edge*. Harcourt Brace & Company, 1997.

Nolan, Han. *If I Should Die Before I Wake*. Harcourt Brace & Company, 1994.

Nolan, Han. *Send Me Down a Miracle*. Harcourt Brace & Company, 1996.

Numeroff, Laura Joffe. *If You Give A Mouse A Cookie.* HarperCollins, 1996.

Park, Barbara. *Mick Harte Was Here.* Alfred A. Knopf, 1995.

Paulsen, Gary. *Hatchet.* Simon & Schuster, 1996.

Rylant, Cynthia. *The Relatives Came.* Simon & Schuster, 1985.

Sendak, Maurice. *Where The Wild Things Are.* HarperCollins, 1988.

Smith, Doris Buchanan. *A Taste of Blackberries.* HarperCollins, 1988.

Smith, Robert Kimmel. *War With Grandpa.* Bantam Doubleday Dell, 1984.

Steig, William. *SHREK!* Farrar, Straus & Giroux, 1990.

Stevenson, James. *I Meant To Tell You.* Greenwillow Books, 1996.

Turner, Ann. *Dakota Dugout.* Simon & Schuster, 1985.

White, E.B. *Charlotte's Web.* HarperCollins, 1974.

Yolen, Jane. *Owl Moon.* Putnam Publishing Group, 1987.